A Faithful Band of Workers

The Beginnings of Churches of Christ in Jackson County, Alabama

John Chisholm Church History Series

C. Wayne Kilpatrick

A Faithful Band of Workers: The Beginnings of Churches of Christ in Jackson County, Alabama

Copyright © 2024 by C. Wayne Kilpatrick

Manufactured in the United States

Cataloging-in-Publication Data

Kilpatrick, C. Wayne (Charlie Wayne), 1943–

A Small Band of Brethren: The Beginnings of Churches of Christ in Jackson County, Alabama / by C. Wayne Kilpatrick

John Chisholm Church History Series

p. cm.

Includes name index.

ISBN: 978-1-956811-73-5 (hdbk); 978-1-956811-74-2 (ebook)

1. Churches of Christ—History—Alabama—Jackson County. 2. Churches of Christ—History—Alabama—Tennessee Valley counties. 3. Churches of Christ—History—Alabama—19th century. I. Author. II. Title. III. Series. 286.676195 DDC20

Cover design by Brittany Vander Maas and Brad McKinnon

Heritage Christian University Press

PO Box HCU
3625 Helton Drive
Florence, Alabama 35630

www.hcu.edu/publications

Contents

FOREWORD

Sunday lunch in the home of Kelby and Martha Smith was where the Harps were first impressed upon by Wayne and Brenda Kilpatrick. After four and a half years in the mission field of New Zealand, my young family made its way to Florence, Alabama, in the winter of 1985-86 to attend International Bible College (now Heritage Christian University). Wayne was to be one of my professors. His expertise is in the fields of history and the Bible. That spring semester, it was my privilege to sit in his World History II class. With every passing day, it was apparent that Wayne's passion was all things historical. On the first day, he said, "We must always stop and pay respects to the bridges we have crossed." And, for the next thirteen weeks, he filled the air with the stories of the past. To Wayne, it was not just information on a page that needed to be shared; it was not just the former things that needed retelling. To him, and ultimately to those of us at his feet, it was our past, our story—our history. Whether talking about John Tetzel's sales of indulgences to build Leo X's St. Peter's Cathedral in Rome, Italy, or the rise of Oliver Cromwell's Parliamentarians in the defeat of Charles I of England, we were led through a maze of factual details that resonated and gave more profound meaning to our lives.

Charlie Wayne Kilpatrick was born on Possum Creek, near Center Hill, Lauderdale County, Alabama, on December 30, 1943. He became a Christian under the preaching of Alden Hendrix, being baptized by him in 1957. After two years of undergraduate studies at the University of North Alabama, Wayne was drafted into the U.S. Air Force. Before his international assignment, he took the opportunity to continue his education by taking courses at the University of Maryland. At the height of the Vietnam War, it was not long before he was stationed in England's R.A.F. Welford in Berkshire, where he was assigned the task of ammunition inspector. During his term of service, he attained the level of sergeant. Being a history lover in an old country like England afforded him a goldmine of antiquity to examine firsthand. Whenever leave was extended, he was either playing his banjo somewhere in a show with some of his friends or striking out on his own in a planned direction to investigate Britain's ancient culture.

Returning to the U.S. after his term of service, Wayne was employed for 18 months by the Tennessee Valley Authority. He married the former Brenda Elaine Chaney of Leighton, Alabama, on December 12, 1970. At the encouragement of his brother-in-law, Milton Chaney, a gospel preacher, Wayne entered the first class of International Bible College (now Heritage Christian University) in the spring of 1972. He was part of the college's first class since transitioning from the older Southeastern Institute of the Bible. After graduating with his Bachelor's Degree in Bible in 1974, Wayne determined to return to England as a missionary. Working primarily with the Wembley church of Christ in Middlesex, just northeast of London, he and Brenda evangelized in that region. Due to a lack of sufficient support, after a year, the family returned to the Shoals area.

Upon his return, he became aware of a need for someone to teach some courses at his alma mater. In the fall of 1975, he accepted the offer to teach World History, Bible Geography, and

Church History at H.C.U. Quickly learning the need for more education, he started taking courses at Harding Graduate School of Religion (now Harding School of Theology) in Memphis, Tennessee. While there, he was privileged to sit at the feet of the noted church historian Earl Irvin West. Wayne completed his studies there with a Master of Arts and Religion (M.A.R.) degree. Over subsequent years, he took twelve post-graduate hours at the University of Alabama and six graduate hours at the University of North Alabama.

The summer following my first class in World History, it was my pleasure to travel with Wayne Kilpatrick to Newport, Wales, UK, where he directed an evangelistic campaign. For a week in the summer of 1986, we knocked on doors, conducted Bible studies in the city during the day, and worshipped with our Welsh brethren in the evenings. One afternoon, we took a break and went about five miles out of town to Caerleon, an ancient Roman city. We walked through the excavated ruins of the amphitheater and the military barracks. A few days following the campaign, we traveled to London, where we had the pleasure of having our own tour guide, C. Wayne Kilpatrick. Whether at the tower of London, Stonehenge, the cathedrals of Winchester, Canterbury, and Salisbury, and just about everywhere in between, the sheer volume of information that seemed to spill freely from this man's mind was nothing short of phenomenal.

Then, there were Kilpatrick's Church History and Restoration History courses. The names, dates, and stories of the past flowed in graceful order from his lips as if he were walking down memory lane. Wayne had a little yellow box with 4x6 index cards that he used to teach his classes. This coveted container of notes was a veritable treasure trove of knowledge he had collected and shared over the years.

Professor Kilpatrick's classes were a magnet to students. His kind-hearted and sanguine spirit filled every lecture with meaningful material that could be used in our ministry for a lifetime.

Once, while teaching the history of the Restoration Movement, we arrived at class, and he told us to go to our cars and follow him a few miles from the school. He took us over to Chisholm Highway to a little shanty of a house. We followed him to the backyard, where among a few trees was the small Chisholm Cemetery. Wayne had just been lecturing about how Benjamin Lynn came to Madison County, Alabama, as early as 1809 to establish New Testament Christianity there. He had explained that Lynn's daughters had married men with that pioneer spirit, Rachel to Marshall De'Spain and Esther to John Chisholm, Jr. Lynn died in 1814 and was buried somewhere north of present-day Huntsville. After 1816, the family moved into what is now Lauderdale County, the Chisholms to Cypress Creek, north of Florence, and the DeSpains to Waterloo.

As we approached the cemetery, there before our eyes were the graves of John and Esther Chisholm. John's father, John Chisholm, Sr., was also buried there. He had been an agent for Cherokee Indian Chief Doublehead and rented land on his reserve. More importantly, these people were the first New Testament Christians in Lauderdale County, planting a New Testament church on Cypress Creek. Also buried in the cemetery was Dorinda Chisholm Hall, the young wife of Benjamin Franklin Hall, the Christian preacher who came to the region in the fall of 1826, preaching baptism for the remission of sins. Under his influence came the baptisms of Tolbert Fanning, Allen Kendrick, and others at the hands of James E. Matthews.

History is a science. With this visit to Chisholm Cemetery, pure science—the ideals, the concepts, the people, the facts on a page—became applied science—seeing, touching, experiencing. Pure history became applied history! It was a hands-on examination of the evidence of history. Later that semester, other trips were made, such as to Red River Meeting House in Logan County, Kentucky, where the Second Great Awakening in America's religious history began under the preaching of Presbyterian James McGready in 1799. We also made our way up to Cane

Ridge Meeting House in Bourbon County, Kentucky, where the Kentucky Revival reached a crescendo in August 1801. From there, Wayne took us to Bethany, West Virginia, where we witnessed the artifacts, the home, the buildings of Bethany College, and the old mansion that attests to the lives and influences of Thomas and Alexander Campbell. The lectures, the trips, the discussions, and the demeanor made Wayne Kilpatrick the master of his profession.

C. Wayne Kilpatrick is known for his research and journalism. The sheer volume of hours he has spent in front of microfilm and microfiche readers, computer screens, and books in his hands is uncountable. During one Christmas break many years ago, Wayne read the 40 volumes of Alexander Campbell's *Millennial Harbinger*. He has one of the largest book collections of any historian, above 40,000 volumes. He was a staff writer for *The Alabama Restoration Journal*, and his numerous articles appear in many history-related magazines. He has lectured on church history for many churches of Christ, at numerous universities, and other education-based programs across America.

C. Wayne Kilpatrick is an evangelist and successful gospel preacher. He has conducted semi-annual evangelism campaigns through Heritage Christian University in many of the states of the United States and other countries. For 20+ years, he traveled annually to teach Bible and church history short courses in the Yucatan, Mexico.

After assisting the History Department at Heritage Christian University for 48 years, he received emeritus status in 2022. At the end of this year, he plans to retire from his position to focus on researching and writing on Alabama restoration history.

This tome is a testimony to the tenacity and pure devotion of the man. After reading it, this writer has been impressed by the voluminous sources gleaned to make this work possible. I fully commend C. Wayne Kilpatrick for this book, as it will be most appreciated by researchers of the future when they attempt to dig where he dug. It will be a much-prized resource of Restoration History in North Alabama for generations to come.

Scott Harp
TheRestorationMovement.com
May 17, 2024

PREFACE

For many years there has been a great need for a comprehensive history of the development of the Restoration Movement in Alabama, and the Tennessee River Valley in general. F. D. Srygley's *Larimore And His Boys* was the earliest attempt to capture any semblance of early Lauderdale County Restoration History, although it was only a partial to the whole of this study. Interest began to manifest itself in the early 1900s. In 1903 A. R. Moore presented a historical review to the Alabama State Board of Missionary Society. This was the first work of its kind, but it was written for the Disciples of Christ—keep in mind that the Disciples were still connected to our movement until 1906. This review was never published. In 1906 J. Waller Henry wrote "Sketches of Pioneer Times" for the *Alabama Christian*—a Disciple paper. Richard L. James and Donald A. Nunnelly wrote graduate theses on the Alabama Restoration Movement. In 1965 George and Mildred Watson published *History of the Christian Churches in the Alabama Area*. All of the above-mentioned material dealt with the Disciples of Christ part of the Restoration Movement. It was not until the 1940s that Asa M. Plyler began traveling over the state and collecting material on the early and then present-day Churches of Christ. He covered every county in the state. His manuscript was finally published upon the request of his family. The book was titled *Historical Sketches of the Churches of Christ in Alabama* and no date of publication was given. Plyler's book gave us some "personally collected information; but beyond that, it has not been of much help, as most of his sources were very limited. Today these sources are more readily available, and we have taken advantage of them.

It was needful—yes even imperative that lives of devotion to the Lord's Kingdom, such as the men and women in this study be told. Younger generations need to know what they have. They need to know that these precious servants of the Lord sacrificed so much so we could be where we are today in the Churches of Christ. A generation, now in danger of squandering away the church, needs to appreciate the fact that many of these subjects went without proper clothing, or proper medical attention many times, were constantly in need of financial means, and made many other sacrifices in order to establish the Lord's work in so many places. It would be the greatest act of ungratefulness toward the generations of these preaching brethren, who gave so much sacrificial devotion to helping save the lost and dying world if their story remains in obscurity. We truly are standing on the shoulders of giants, and these—our predecessors were the giants.

We have undertaken the task of producing a history that uses only documented sources—such as church records, journal articles, unpublished autobiographies, documented papers written for schools and universities, published and unpublished interviews, courthouse records, and even monuments and cemeteries. We have limited this study to the four Alabama counties north of the Tennessee River. That is where the Alabama Restoration Movement began.

This book is written to be used, hopefully, as a resource tool to encourage further research into local church histories. Perhaps, the lives of these forefathers in the Lord's work may inspire us to do great things for our Lord and Savior Jesus Christ.

Introduction

The four counties that lie on the north bank of the Tennessee River—Madison, Jackson, Lauderdale, and Limestone—will be the subject under consideration for this work. We will treat the counties chronologically in the order in which the Restoration Movement began.

At first, Alabama was part of the Mississippi Territory, which was ceded by Georgia and South Carolina to the United States. The Territory of Mississippi was an organized incorporated territory of the United States that existed from April 7, 1798, until December 10, 1817, when the western half of the territory was admitted to the Union as the State of Mississippi and the eastern half became the Alabama Territory until its admittance to the Union as the State of Alabama on December 14, 1819.

Prior to the War of 1812, many settlers came into what is now Madison and Jackson Counties, Alabama. Alabama was then still part of the Mississippi Territory. They could not legally, nor safely travel any further into what is presently known as Northwest Alabama because the Indians controlled the land until 1816. Some of these pioneers settled in northeastern Jackson County near modern day Bridgeport, Alabama. another group settled 10 miles north of Huntsville, Alabama, and established Meridianville.

In the years that followed the close of the War of 1812, an influx of thousands of settlers came into the northern part of Alabama from Tennessee, North and South Carolina, Georgia, and Virginia. This was due to the promise of bounty lands to be given to men who had fought in the War of 1812. With each new settler came his own peculiar religious views, resulting in the founding of churches to propagate their views. Along with these settlers from the older states came the views of Barton Stone, James O'Kelly, and a few years later, Alexander Campbell. Just as with other religious groups, the followers of Stone, O'Kelly, and Campbell founded congregations of believers, who were dedicated to spreading the message of the Restoration Movement. Many of these congregations would prosper for a few years and then gradually disappear. Some, however, would weather the storms of time and exist down to the present.

In Northeast Alabama, the Bridgeport (Rocky Springs) and Meridianville pioneers were neither of the James O'Kelley, Barton Warren Stone nor Alexander Campbell groups. These pioneers began their New Testament churches independent of the other movements. Rocky Springs congregation was established in 1811 or 1812 by members of the Old Philadelphia church in Warren County, Tennessee, which had been established by a people who came from a mixture of religious beliefs and who wanted to follow the New Testament pattern They had established their congregation near Viola, Tennessee in 1808. The Gains and Price families moved shortly afterward to Rocky Springs (1811 or 1812). The Meridianville work was begun by Benjamin Lynn in 1808 or 1809. Both groups had studied themselves out of denominationalism without the influence of any of the three above-mentioned movements.

In Northwest Alabama, one such congregation (Stoney Point —established in 1816) has managed to endure. Several other congregations in this area that were established before the Civil

War, were not so durable. Many of them have faded into obscurity.

Much has been written about the political history of this area, but very little has been written about the religious history. Hardly anything has been written concerning the Restoration Movement in North Alabama. F. D. Srygley's biography of T. B. Larimore, *Larimore and His Boys,* sheds some light upon the history of this area and George and Mildred Watson's *History of the Christian Churches in the Alabama Area* gives some insight into this part of the state. Several histories of local congregations have appeared, but many times these works are weighted down by local traditions, rather than historical facts. Due to the lack of knowledge on the part of the average church member concerning the Restoration Movement, the purpose of this study is to give a historical account of the North Alabama movement. Our method shall be to discover who established these works and what caused them to grow or die, whichever the case may be. Since every historical work must have a beginning and an end, we have set the date of our study to begin with 1808–1809, the approximate time Benjamin Lynn came to Madison County, Alabama, and ending with the year 1914, the year World War I began. This time span covers a little over a hundred years of Alabama restoration history. It should be remembered, however, that this is in no way a complete history because there are examples of churches, such as Liberty, which appeared in *The Christian Register* of 1848 as being in Lauderdale County, Alabama, having eighty-five members, and possessing their own house of worship, then disappearing from all written records. Such incidents make it impossible to compile a complete history. History, however, does not dwell upon that which has been lost, but rather that which can be found. This historical study shall be based upon only what can be found.

To prepare such historical undertaking many sources have been consulted. Local newspapers of the period under discussion, local courthouse records, journals of historical societies, unpublished histories, and biographical sketches have been valuable sources of material. Many books have been written by our brethren on subjects not related to the Alabama area, yet touching upon it, and literature by other religious groups have proven helpful. There are several historical collections of the brotherhood that have supplied valuable aid in this investigation, but the chief source of material has been found in brotherhood journals beginning with Campbell's first issue of *The Christian Baptist* in 1823, through most major journals until the year 2000. Where occasion has demanded and opportunity has afforded, different portions of North Alabama have been visited and much valuable information has been gained by private conversation. Such were the sources from whence this history is derived. It is hoped that this uncovering of information will give a better understanding of the Churches of Christ in North Alabama.

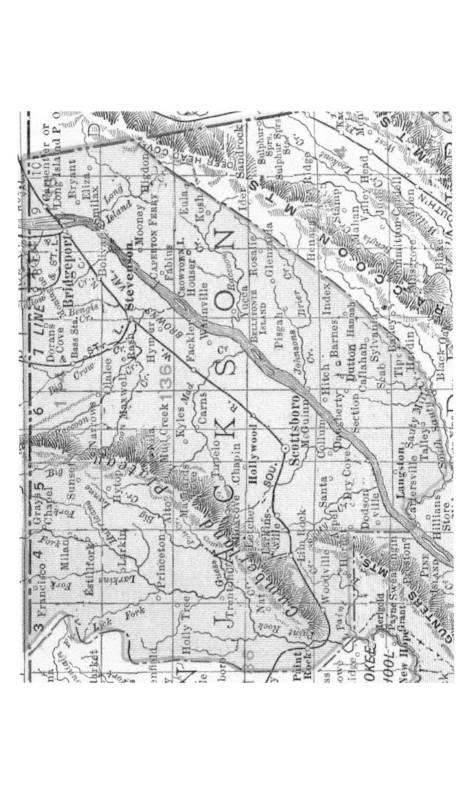

JACKSON

When Jackson County was created in 1819, Sauta Cave was established as the temporary seat of justice, but shortly thereafter it was moved to the village of Sauta located near Birdsong Spring. In 1828, county records were moved into the new brick, two-story courthouse in Bellefonte which served as the county seat for 40 years. In 1859, a county election was held to determine whether a new courthouse should be more centrally located in Stevenson or Scottsboro. Stevenson was chosen, but the Civil War nullified this action, and the matter was not settled until 1868. On September 5, 1868, the Commissioners Court met in Bellefonte and voted to remove the county seat from Bellefonte to Scottsboro, named for its founder Robert T. Scott, a native of North Carolina. In November 1868, county records were moved from Bellefonte to a small brick house in Scottsboro rented by Probate Judge David Tate.

ANTIOCH—ROCKY SPRING

The earliest work in Jackson County, Alabama was about a mile due west of Bridgeport, Alabama. This was the Antioch congregation relocated and renamed Rocky Springs.[1] Before we begin with the actual work at Antioch, we must first begin with a work that began in Warren County, Tennessee—known as the Old Philadelphia Church of Christ.

Early in the 1800's several Presbyterian and Episcopalian pioneers had moved from North Carolina and Virginia into the Tennessee River Valley and adjoining areas of Tennessee, some of them founding a community in Warren County, which became known as Old Philadelphia. These were religious people without a preacher, and they studied the scriptures together. Soon they were worshipping as one body, calling themselves Christians and the church only as the church of Christ.

Among this group were four brothers, Elisha, John, Hugh, and William J. Price who came from Ireland and settled in Asheville, North Carolina, and later moved to Hickory Creek. Elisha was the eldest, born in 1770. He died in 1876, two days after he reached his 106th birthday.

A post road from Knoxville to New Orleans was opened in 1805 and some six or seven years later, when the territory of

Alabama, then largely occupied by the Cherokee Indians, was opened to white settlers, among the first to arrive and settle in Northern Alabama was a group from Warren County, Tennessee. Some of these people located near the post road and established a community that they called Antioch. This was early in 1811, and before Jackson County was created. Among these were William J. Price, baptized in 1811 at Old Philadelphia, Tennessee, and his wife and a slave named Moses. Major William D. Gaines was also in this group. They selected a home site near a spring they found by following a game trial and named the place Rocky Springs. It was a little over a mile south of Antioch. W. J. Price was a prominent leader in the church until his death.[2]

Price's gravestone in the Rocky Springs Cemetery has this inscription:

William J. Price
Born January 15, 1793
Died January 26, 1868.

A community grew up around the home of William J. Price, on the post road to Rocky Springs. A post office was established there, along with an Indian Trading Post, a tavern, and stables for changing horses on the stagecoaches. On June 12, 1847, the congregation moved into a new building at Rocky Springs, abandoning the old one at Antioch. At that time there were eighty-two members.

Very little has been recorded of the Rocky Springs history from 1811 until the appearance of Benjamin Franklin Hall, who had been heavily influenced by Barton Warren Stone from Cane Ridge, Kentucky.

Before we relate Hall's story of his first meeting at Antioch, we are compelled to give an account that was related by Hall of an incident that occurred in 1825 in Jackson County, Alabama. This incident occurred a few miles south of Antioch in the Bellefonte community. It had been told to him by Samuel Rogers who was an eyewitness to the scene. Rogers was one of B. W. Stone's co-workers. This account will help set the stage for the Jackson County Restoration Movement. The story went as follows:

> An incident was related to me by the brother Rogers above mentioned, and of which he was an eye and ear witness, being at the time a Methodist, and present in the tent when it occurred.
>
> A Methodist minister of the name of Mr. XXXX had been sent among the Cherokee Indians who lived at that time [1825] just across the Tennessee River from Jackson County, Ala. for the purpose of distributing Bibles and Testaments among them. Seeing an intelligent looking young who could read English, he made him a present of a New Testament, requesting him at the same time to read it and to do as it told him. The Indian accepted the present and promised to comply with the preacher's request. This was early in the spring of 1825. In the autumn of the same year the Methodists held a camp meeting in Jackson County, Ala. near Bellefonte. The young Indian hearing of the meeting went over to it. On reaching the campground, he inquired for Col. U., the preacher above mentioned. He was informed that he was in the Preacher's tent, which was pointed out to him, He was at once admitted, and, recognizing the preacher, offered him his hand, telling him at the same time he was the man to whom he had given the New Testament; and he added: "I have done as you requested. I have read the book and have come to get you to go with me to the river." "Why?" the preacher inquired, "Do you want me to go with you to the river?" "I want you to baptize me," was the answer of the red man. "I can baptize you without going to the river," responded the preacher. "How?" the Indian asked. The preacher proceeded to tell him; he "would take some water in a tumble and pour it on his head." This information took the Indian all aback. He paused a moment in evident perplexity and doubt, his eyes resting on the ground. Then raising his head and fixing his keen dark eyes on the preacher,

he asked: "Is that baptism?" "Yes," responded the preacher, "that is the way we baptize." The Indian stood a moment as if in deep thought; then raising his head and fixing his eyes again on the preacher, he said, "Col. if that is baptism, you gave me the wrong book!" This terminated the interview. The disappointed Indian instantly left the place and returned to his home.[3]

Bellefonte was an annual gathering place between Indians and the white folk who lived in the vicinity. It also brought a host of ministers of all persuasions to the valley. That is why Samuel Rogers, who lived in Cynthiana, Kentucky came all the way to Jackson County, Alabama. He was there observing and preaching. This reveals that our brethren were already coming into Jackson at an early date. The road from Lexington, Kentucky to Florence, Alabama branched into several roads that eventually converged in the Tennessee Valley and came into Florence as two roads—the Nashville Road and the Huntsville-Florence Road. Hall and the other brethren who came into Jackson County, Alabama traveled the branch that left McMinnville, Tennessee, and traveled by Old Philadelphia and came down Monteagle mountain to where Sewanee is located and turned eastward coming into the northern part of Jackson County, Alabama. That would bring them into the Antioch community.

This was Hall's route into Alabama. Hall's next meeting was at Antioch in August 1826. It was also his first trip to Antioch. He described the meeting in his autobiography:

Our next meeting was in the upper edge of Jackson County, Ala. in what was called the Price neighborhood. Here again I preached the ancient gospel and immersed for remission of sins some twenty-three persons, among them a James C. Anderson and a brother Russell. They had both been Methodists. Brother Anderson soon became a preacher; and for many years labored through both Ala. and Tenn. He was an efficient preacher and won many souls to God. He was blind in one eye. He now rests from his labors.[4]

The work at Antioch (Rocky Springs) was growing increasingly spiritually and numerically. James Clark Anderson began working in the Lord's kingdom almost immediately. This is confirmed by a certificate of approbation issued six months later to Anderson on February 12, 1827. The certificate reads as follows:

> This may certify to all whom it may concern, that our beloved Brother James Anderson is authorized to preach the word of truth wherever he may have opportunity by approbation of the congregation at Antioch, of which he is a faithful member.
>
> Signed: Elisha Price
> William King
> Andrew Russell
> Elders, Church of Christ
> at Antioch.[5]

This empowered Anderson to preach but he could not perform weddings. In other words, he was in a trial period, which was common in those days.

In July of that year, brethren from Kentucky, Tennessee, and Alabama met at Antioch, (which was in Jackson County, Alabama) for a conference. This list of ministers, who attended was published in Barton Warren Stone's *Christian Messenger*. James C. Anderson was listed as an attendee and as an unordained minister. James E. Matthews of Florence, Alabama gave the report:

FLORENCE AUGUST 18, 1827.

DEAR BROTHER, — Our annual meeting commenced at Antioch, Jackson county, Ala. on Thursday, 26th of July 1827, under the most convincing evidence of divine favor, and continued until the 31st, at 1 o'clock. During that period, there were devotional exercises, in some way, almost without intermission. I have been trying to preach 20 years, have attended many Conferences and Camp meetings, but thankfully acknowledge the one at Antioch, far surpassed anything of the kind I ever beheld. Prejudice, partyism and sin, seemed to fall prostrate before the Ark of God, while the assembled multitudes were pierced to the heart with the darts of truth. The laboring brethren seemed to have lost sight of defending the truth, and to content themselves with letting the truth defend them.

Multitudes professed faith in Jesus, and about 30 were baptized in his name. I had the pleasure of administering the supper on the Lord's day, about 10 o'-clock, P. M. It was one of the most heavenly scenes I ever witnessed— there were about 600 communants. At the close of the meeting, it was not easy to find a non-professor on the encampment, and what few remained, seemed to be buried in distress, like those returning from the internment of their friends.

Conference sat on Monday. The Lord being our law giver, has kindly saved us the labor of legislating; of course, we had but little to do, only to make the necessary arrangements for the execution of his laws, and the administration of his word, in which the brethren appeared entirely cordial. We thought it proper to limit our conference to the bounds of our state. It is the wish of the brethren that there be a general Conference, for the purpose of a more general union & uniform understanding. Our Conference, and meeting throughout, was expressive of the most perfect harmony. — Our next Conference will be held at Hurricane, Madison county the first Lord's day in February 1828. I subjoin the names of the preachers belonging to this Conference.

ORDAINED. — Elisha Price, John H. Parkhill, Elisha Randolph, Mansel W. Matthews, John M'Daniel, Thacker V.

Griffin, Isaac Mulkey, William Clap, Crocket M'Daniel, Robert Baits, Jonathan Wallis, James E. Matthews, Reuben Mardis, E. D. Moore.

UNORDAINED. — James Anderson. Lorenzo D. Griffen, Jonathan G. Ward, Wm. J. Price, Wm. W. Wilson, Andrew Russel, Jonathan Parker.[6]

We notice that Elisha Price was listed as an ordained minister and his brother William J. Price was an unordained minister in attendance at Antioch. Ordination was simply a formality required by state governments when it came to legally recognized weddings. This was to protect against fake preachers coming into a community and posing as a bona fide preacher to make money from the weddings performed.

The next year he was ordained to preach the gospel. A fragile old original copy of his "Ordination Certificate" has been preserved in the Anderson family records. The certificate reads as follows:

> Be it remembered that on the 4th day of February 1828 our Beloved James Anderson was publicly and solemnly set apart for the work of the Ministry by the imposition of the hand of the Presbytery.
>
>   Given Under Our Hands
>   E.D. Moore, E.C.C.
>   John Langley.[7]

The E. D. Moore, who signed the certificate, was Ephraim D. Moore of Florence, Alabama. Moore was the first minister to move into Lauderdale County. He worked there until he moved to North-East Texas to work for the remainder of his life.

To highlight the ordination certificate question, we turn to James C. Anderson again. 1829 finds Anderson on preaching tours in Limestone County, Alabama. An entry in the Marriage Book states the following:

State of Alabama:
County Court Clerk of Limestone County, October 26, 1829.
This day James Anderson produced here in open court a
certificate setting forth he is an ordained minister of the Gospel
and in regular communion with the church of Christ. It is
therefore ordered by the court that the same James Anderson be
licensed to celebrate the rites of matrimony, in the state agreeably
to the laws of said state.[8]

The court under the hand of Robert Austin, Jr., gave
Anderson leave to perform weddings. This illustrates that James
Clark Anderson was as faithful in the Lord's work as Hall had
described him in his autobiography.

The above two certificates were found by William Anderson,
who was president of Nashville Bible School, which later became
David Lipscomb College. David Lipscomb and William
Anderson attended the fifty-fifth anniversary, in 1902, of Rocky
Springs having moved from Antioch to Rocky Springs in 1847.
Lipscomb wrote of this celebration and how William had found
his father's certificates:

> We spent Sunday, June 15, with the church at Rock Spring,
> Jackson County, Ala. The occasion was the fifty-fifth anniver-
> sary of the planting of the church at that place. This was what
> they claimed and is as far back as their records reach; but Brother
> William Anderson's father was reared in that section of country,
> had been a member of the church of Christ in that county, and
> began preaching there, and he concluded to attend this meeting
> to see If he could learn something more of his father's early days
> and work. Brother Anderson had found among his father's
> papers two certificates ....[9]

This information by David Lipscomb confirms the authen-
ticity of the two ordination certificates of James Clark Anderson.

By 1832 emphasis had shifted to another location in Jackson

County. The annual meeting was held at Lewis, Jackson County, Alabama on the 5th Lord's day in July [1832].[10] The list for the annual meeting in 1834 was also at Lewis. That was the site chosen for the "CAMP MEETING APPOINTMENTS FOR 1834."[11] Just where the location of Lewis' was in Jackson is unknown to the writer currently.

By June 12, 1847, the congregation had relocated about a mile south near a large spring from which the new location took the name—Rocky Springs. In 1864 the Union Army destroyed the Rocky Springs building. The congregation refused to disband so, they began meeting again in the old Antioch building and continued to worship there until August 1867, when a new building was completed at Rocky Springs. After moving into the new meeting house, on August 5, 1867, elders were chosen. They were J. H. J. Williams and J. B. Arendale. W. D. McCampbell was appointed as deacon and three sisters were appointed as deaconesses. W. J. Hughes, a nephew of William J. Price, was appointed clerk and treasurer. (Flyer printed for the two-hundred-year celebration of the church at Rocky Springs.) The celebration was based on the wrong year (1807) as the year of establishment for the Rocky Springs congregation. The men who established the Antioch-Rocky Springs congregation were still living in Warren County, Tennessee until 1811 or 1812.

The first published report after the Civil War was a report by Washington Bacon. Prior to the end of the war, little information could be found. Bacon's report which was published in the *Gospel Advocate* in May gave a sad report. Bacon reported on the destitute condition of the church at Rocky Springs. We give the report in full:

> Trenton, GA., April 23, 1867, Bro. Lipscomb: A few days ago, I was in Jackson County, Alabama, near Bridgeport, where there is a congregation of brethren worshipping at Rocky Springs and their condition is truly distressing. There are ten widows with

thirty-five children, which are needing bread and meat and also old Bro. William Price and his sister wife, who heretofore were the pillow and stay or Rocky Springs Congregation, are now in a state of entire dependence. He himself is in a state of paralysis, and entirely helpless, and has to be waited on day and night, by Bro. William Hughes, or some member of his family. If aid can be had, extend it to them. I will write to you again in a few days. Your brother in the Lord, Washington Bacon.[12]

This report almost brings one to tears to see the suffering caused by the Civil War and the sad condition of Brother W. J. Price. In July Bacon sent the second report, which he had promised in the first report. This report was given on a happier note. It read:

Trenton, GA., July 22, 1867. Bros Fanning and Lipscomb: After my respects, I say to you that on the fourth Lord's day in June at my appointment at Mt. Laurel, on Sand Mountain that there were two noble accessions to the army of the faithful, and also on the first lord's day in this inst., at Rocky Springs in Jackson county, Alabama, aided by Bro. Joseph Wheeler, who did good service in the Master's cause, there were here others, and at Liberty, in this county, the third Lord's day one other, making in all since my last writing six. To the Lord be all praise. Now as ever, your brother in hope of eternal life, Washington Bacon.[13]

In the above report, Bacon mentions Joseph Wheeler, who would also become an asset to the congregation at Rocky Springs. He would make many trips to Rocky Springs in the next few years. Bacon also made the next report. He wrote on August 19, 1867:

Bros. Fanning and Lipscomb: I left home on Friday before the first Lord's day, last, for Rocky Springs, Jackson county, Ala. I preached for the brethren on Saturday and Lord's day, and set in order the things that were wanting, and closed with one addition ....[14]

The year 1867 was a very good year for the church at Rocky Springs—spiritually speaking. Rocky Springs began to take on a new life. It had several preachers who began to come to the congregation. In January 1868 Washington Bacon authored a report that read as follows:

> Brother Lipscomb: It has occurred to me that, although I have given you in scraps, the success of the Gospel in my field of labor for the year that has just passed and gone, that it would be nothing amiss to condense the whole. At the commencement of the year, my broken-down circumstances were such that I thought I would confine my labors exclusively to my immediate neighborhood and preach for and to the three congregations in this county as I had no horse to ride and did so for a time. And having a little business on the west side of the Tennessee river in the neighborhood of Rocky Spring, Jackson county, Alabama, the brethren at that place earnestly solicited me to visit them and preach for them. I told them that I had no horse; Bro. William Hughes proposed to pay my fare on the railroad, if I would preach for them. I thanked him for his liberal proposition and told him, as we were all broken down by the war, to keep his money for other purposes, and as soon as I could make it convenient, I would visit them. So, I added that point to my field, a distance of twenty-three miles, walking all the while. But after my crop of corn was finished, I then extended my labors down as low as Calhoun county, Ala., the result of which has been one hundred and fifty-eight to the army of the faithful, and the organization of four congregations. To the Lord be all the praise ... Washington Bacon.[15]

This report, as can be seen, was published on February 6th. Bacon gave a good insight into how he came to associate with Rocky Springs. In July he reported again on his work with the church at Rocky Springs:

> Scottsboro, Ala., July 13, 1868. Brother Lipscomb, It has been so long since I have written to you that I have forgotten the date of my last writing I recollect, though; that I then reported the success of the Gospel in my field of labor. But as it has not been published in the Gospel Advocate, I thought it would be nothing amiss to write to you this morning and give you a state-ment of the success of the truth of the Gospel in my field of labor, up to this writing. I commenced my year's labor at Rocky Spring, Jackson county, Ala., the first Lord's Day in March; but the high waters in the months of April and May prevented me from visiting all the congregations that I visit this year.[16]

During his new labor with Rocky Springs, Washington Bacon gave another report on Rocky Springs in October 1869, and it was printed in December. His work at Rocky Springs was accomplishing much good for the Lord's kingdom as is demonstrated by his following report:

> At my protracted meeting at Rocky Spring, in this County, I was met by Bros. Wheeler and Stone, at which point they labored faithfully till Monday noon at which time Bro. Wheeler had to leave to meet other engagements, and Bro. Stone remaining we prosecuted the meeting till Thursday noon. Closing with twelve additions, two from the Primitive Baptists, one from the Missionary Baptists, three from the Methodists, and six from the world ... Washington Bacon.[17]

The Wheeler that was mentioned in the above report was Joseph Wheeler who was close friends with Washington Bacon and preached, essentially, in the same congregations as Bacon did. They preached on a circuit in which they would preach at one or two congregations per weekend and then move on to another congregation on the circuit. That is the way most of the pioneer country preachers operated. The Stone who was mentioned was Brother G. B. Stone of Bradley County, East Tennessee (Cleveland area). He often came to the Rocky Springs community and held meetings.

We have a glimpse into the congregation in 1870. A gospel meeting was held there in 1870, but the preacher is unknown to us. The only information we have on this meeting is contained in the following obituary:

> Died near Bridgeport, Jackson county, Ala., Sallie Ally and Ida Hughes. Sallie was born March 10, 1857, and died April 6, 1885. She obeyed the gospel at Rocky Springs, in 1870. Ida was born June 15, 1861. obeyed the gospel at Rocky Springs in 1870, died April 25, 1885. These two sisters lived obedient lives from the time they obeyed the Gospel until the day of their death. As our sisters loved the cause and were always at their posts, we will miss them. But our loss is their gain. Their suffering is over. They leave a host of relations to mourn their loss. But dry your tears, dear friends, and prepare to meet them. "We sorrow not as those that have no hope" B. C. Goodwin.[18]

This obituary revealed that Rocky Springs had gained into their fold, two precious ladies the same year and perhaps at the very same meeting. It also revealed that the church lost the same two precious ladies in the same month in 1885. This is unusual because Sallie was 28 years old, and Ida was 24 years of age. Perhaps some kind of disease was rampant in the community. We may never know, but a sad picture has been revealed in this double obituary of two precious members at Rocky Springs.

The above report was given in this order to illustrate the event that occurred in 1870. That is why it appears out of chronological order. W. T. Stephens of Larkinsville, Jackson County gave the next report in 1885 that included a small bit about Rocky Springs. He just mentioned that B. C. Goodwin preached at Rocky Springs every first Sunday of the month.[19]

The next window into the history at Rocky Springs comes to us through the *Gospel Advocate* by E. H. Boyd. Boyd was circulating in the Jackson—Madison counties area. He was now moving to Jasper, Tennessee which was approximately twelve miles from Rocky Springs. That would enable Boyd to be an asset to the Rocky Springs congregation. The report simply names the congregations with whom Boyd would be working for the following year—1890. He wrote:

> My work for the year 1890 will be at Jasper and South Pittsburg, Tenn., Old Rocky Springs, Ala., and perhaps Cowan, Tenn., and wherever these congregations may please to send me. I love the loyalty of the Gospel Advocate and as soon as Γ am through moving will try to add a few names to her list of readers. Success to you and much love to all your contributors and readers. E. H. Boyd. Pikeville.[20]

Boyd reported on a meeting he held at Rocky Springs two years later:

> Jasper, Sept. 12, '92. — I began a meeting at Old Rocky Springs, near Bridge port. Ala., on the fourth Lord's day in August, continuing until Friday which resulted in ten additions to the army of the faithful. Audiences and interest good. E. H. Boyd. [21]

Boyd reports in the *Gospel Advocate* again in December of 1893, when he gives a short report on the work at Rocky Springs. He wrote:

Jasper. One baptized at Old Rocky Springs on the third Lord's day in November. I shall do all I can to circulate your literature. E. H. Boyd.[22]

It would be another two years before another report would come forth. We, therefore, have approximately two years of silence with no published report on the work at Rocky Springs. He gave an explanation, perhaps, explaining why the silence. His health was in peril. He explained in the following report:

> Jasper, March 6. I came out of the protracted work last fall completely broken down in health with meetings and appointments before me that I was not able to meet. I have been in poor health all winter, but since the middle of January have been trying to meet appointments, and have done so thus far, but my health continues to be very little improved, and I fear I shall be compelled to give up my work altogether. I am preaching once a month at the following points: Tracy City, Rocky Springs, Ala., Bridgeport, Ala., Crow Creek, Ala., and Bethel, Tenn. At all of these points I find more than usual interest manifested and a more effectual working in the measure or every part of the body, which makes the outlook for the future of these churches hopeful for additions and growth in grace as well. Brethren pray for me, for verily the fields are white unto harvest, and the laborers few. E. H. Boyd.[23]

Even though the next report is discussed slightly out of chronological order; we give it in this order because Boyd's health is under discussion. This report gives a bleak picture of Boyd's health and explains why J. H. Morton wrote as he did:

> Brother E. H. Boyd, of Jasper, Tenn., stopped a few hours at Bridgeport, on his return from Crow Creek, his regular appointment. One was baptized by him there. Brother Boyd is an old-fashioned gospel preacher. He has been in feeble health for some

time. but we are glad to report that he is now improving. May the Lord bless the faithful in Christ everywhere! J. H. Morton. [24]

The next report was made by J. H. Morton and is given in the proper chronological order. He came and held a meeting in August of 1896. His report gave a good picture of Rocky Springs for that year. It read:

Bridgeport, Aug; 27. On Friday, Aug. 14, we left our home (near Berlin, Tenn.), and boarded a train for Bridgeport, Ala. Arriving at Bridgeport, we were met at the train by Brother J. R. Johnson, who furnished us conveyance to his home, near Rocky Spring Church. We commenced our meeting at Rocky Springs on Saturday night, August 16, and continued the meeting ten days, resulting in twenty-four additions from different sources. The meeting closed with good interest. Two confessed the Savior on the last night of the meeting. We had promised only eighteen days preaching in Jackson County. Ala. Doran's Cove claimed the balance of our time. Brother J. R. Johnson led the song service, and did all the baptizing during the meeting, The following preachers cheered us by their presence, and gave us their assistance in the song and prayer service: Old Father Daniels, of Scottsboro, Ala.; J. R. Johnson. J. H. Masengale, H. L. Taylor. C. W. Hall, A. N. Foshee, of Jackson County. We began at Doran's Cove last night. One was baptized. today. J. H. Morton.[25]

He gave another report at about the same time as the above one which stated:

Bridgeport, Aug. 19. I am now in a meeting at old Rocky Spring, Jackson County, Ala. This is the fourth day of our meeting, and there have been sixteen additions from all sources up to date. The crowds are large, and the interest is fine. I will go from here to Doran's Cove, Ala., embracing the fifth Lord's day in August. J. H. Morton.[26]

Morton further reported on the meeting and gave more information on Rocky Springs and the Jackson County work. In December one of the former members at Rocky Spring died, and his obituary was published in the *Gospel Advocate*. It revealed more information about Rocky Springs:

Died, at his home in Bridgeport, Jackson County, Ala., June 10, 1896, Brother W. L. McFarlin. He was born one and one-half miles from where he lived and died. He was born November 16, 1827. He was married to Miss Judith E. Price in 1853, who became the mother of his only surviving son, R. A. McFarlin. After her death he married Miss Mary E. Hughes, who survives him. Brother McFarlin was stricken with paralysis on September 12, 1895. After several months he partially recovered, but never fully regained his health. He was knocked down by a large swinging gate, from the effects of which he died. He obeyed the gospel in the year 1847 and was in the first organization of the Rocky Spring congregation, one of the oldest Christian organizations in the county. At the organization at Bridgeport, in 1893, he was chosen one of the elders, and we all looked on him as the man of our counsel, he being the senior. Though not gifted to lead in public service, he earnestly contended for the faith. Our brother was a true Christian, of a social and loving disposition, a good neighbor, a loving father, and a faithful companion. Brother L. R. Sewell was with us in a protracted meeting at the time of his death and conducted the devotional services in a most solemn and impressive manner. Bridgeport, Ala. H. L. Taylor.[27]

He was valuable to two congregations and had a part in their organization. Both Rocky Springs and Bridgeport benefited from his wisdom and leadership. Taylor said of him:

He obeyed the gospel in the year 1847 and was in the first organization of the Rocky Spring congregation, one of the oldest Christian organizations in the county. At the organization at Bridgeport, in 1893, he was chosen one of the elders ....[28]

Following McFarlin's obituary, the next information comes in November 1897. It was short but to the point:

The meeting at Rock Spring, Jackson County, Ala., embracing the fourth Sunday in October was one of much interest. Brother Granville Lipscomb was compelled to leave on Friday to meet another engagement; Brothers Willie Lloyd and J. R. Johnson continued it. Up to Thursday night there were seven additions. [29]

This is the first visit by a member of the Lipscomb family. The visit started out as a good meeting with high expectations, but it ended with a lower key. It still resulted in seven additions.

The work was once again advancing in the cause of Christ. The 1890's, overall, had been good for the church at Rocky Springs.

In 1902 a fifty-fifth-year celebration was held at Rocky Springs — celebrating since the church relocated from the old Antioch site to the new location at Rocky Springs, which was about a mile south of Antioch. David Lipscomb attended this celebration, along with William Anderson, son of James Clark Anderson. Lipscomb authored a lengthy article about this gathering. We give the greater part of his article:

Brother Anderson found that this Antioch Church met in a house only a mile or two from the present Rock(y) Spring(s) church house. [For some Lipscomb was confused as to the correct name of Rocky Springs. It was always "Rocky Springs"] The elders who signed the paper for his father James Anderson, were the ancestors of persons now living in the church there. So, this church was in existence seventy-five years ago and is known as "Antioch Church." They built at the present place fifty-five years ago, and it took its present name from a spring nearby. The records of the church embrace only the meetings at the present place.

Ephraim D. Moore, who signed the second paper as evangelist of the church of Christ was a well-known and well-beloved evangelist of North Alabama. I have heard Brother Fanning speak of him as one to whom he was greatly indebted for ·is early instruction in the word of God. Brother Fanning was baptized by James Matthews, of Mississippi, in October 1827 (1826).[30] Brethren Anderson and Fanning were always intimate fellow-workers in the gospel. Brother Anderson was his senior in the flesh and in the spirit. This is probably the oldest church of Christ in this Southern country, at least the oldest now in existence.

This church probably had its origin some years before the date of these papers, from the preaching of B. W. Stone and his associates, as many churches along the mountain bench in Tennessee and Alabama were planted by these teachers.

The day for celebrating the planting was a beautiful one-cloudy, without rain. An arbor had been erected. I suppose four or five hundred people were present. Brethren from Chattanooga, Tenn.; Trenton, Ga.; Scottsboro, Alabama; and other points in Alabama and Tennessee, were present. We met here our aged brother, A. Brown, of Trenton, Ga —now past his fourscore, a daughter of W. Bacon, a daughter of Joseph Wheeler, and a granddaughter of Madison Love. All three of these brethren were devoted and faithful preachers of the gospel about the middle of the last century. Preaching was had on Saturday night, twice on Sunday, and on Sunday night. Brother Anderson and I spoke twice each. After dinner on Sunday Brother Johnson, the earnest preacher of the congregation, read the original church compact and the names of the members for twenty years after they began meeting at the present place. There were only a few of that number present to answer the roll call. The number that had been enrolled as members during this time reached eight or nine hundred. The community is of the class that ought to produce the best results —composed of neither rich nor poor, but those with moderate means. The church, like most country churches, while maintaining the worship, has never been self-sacrificing and aggressive in spreading the gospel, as churches should be but promises to do better in the future. They are now setting apart the contributions of one Lord's day in the month to be spent in preaching the gospel in destitute places in their county. If this work is persevered in until the county is preached to, there is no danger, but they will reach beyond the county lines. The point for them to watch is to make an earnest and faithful sacrifice on that day that will result in some earnest preaching in destitute places. Do not make the farce of pretending to sacrifice and contribute and do nothing. The time has come-and it is well it has come-when men must be more earnest and faithful in the practice of the Christian duties, or they must give up· their religion.

Rock Spring (Rocky Springs) Church is two miles out from Bridgeport, Ala. The Nashville, Chattanooga and St. Louis Railway and the Memphis and Charleston Railroad cross the Tennessee River at Bridgeport. Here, also, the river crosses, or cuts through, the mountain range that passes through Tennessee into Alabama.

Some years ago, some promoters and capitalists selected this point to build a large city. They graded streets on a magnificent scale, built fine business houses, and a number of dwellings and factories, brought water from a mountain spring, and put in an electric plant to supply lights for a city with thirty thousand people. The city failed to materialize; so, there are a number of large and costly buildings that can be bought cheap-some of them unfinished and going to wreck. It is a good shipping point for mining and manufacturing and may yet grow to a place of importance.

Brethren Grant, Logue, and Gillentine have selected it as a place to open a school. A more picturesque place, with finer views of mountain range, vale, and river we do not know. It is a healthy place. They have secured residences and school building on favorable terms, and we see no reason they should not build up a good school. They have all been with us at the Nashville Bible School—Brother Grant as teacher, Brother Logue as both student and teacher, and Brother Gillentine as student. They are all good men and good teachers and deserve a good school.

Brother Grant was moved by another consideration: he felt that there was an undue proportion of preachers collecting in Nashville, while the country is destitute of them, and that Bridgeport is a good center to occupy, from which they can spread the gospel in the country adjacent. His idea is good in this. Preachers should seek destitute fields instead of those that are well supplied with churches and preachers. I believe it a mistake for a preacher to move to a city when he does. not labor in that city. He greatly buries himself and his personal influence when he locates in a city to labor elsewhere. His personal influence should be a factor in his work that grows with age and supplements the declining fervor, magnetism, and eloquence of his younger days. The idea is prevalent that a preacher must fail at fifty or sixty years of age. This is only when he fails to so live that when his character ripens and mellows with age, he will shed the fragrance of a godly life around him. If he does this, he will not be dependent upon the oratorical and magnetic powers of youth to benefit people. A man who is always moving from place to place or does not live among the people for whom he labors, cannot exert this hallowed and most lasting influence.

I know it is frequently pleaded that the city is the center from which he can more readily go in every direction I do not believe one preacher ought to try to go everywhere or in every direction. There is not a county in Tennessee that does not furnish an ample field for the labors and talent of any one man. The cause of Christ and the preacher would be both helped if he would diligently cultivate the fields around his own home and plant and cultivate a vineyard of which he might eat the fruit. If the twenty-five or thirty preacher m and around Nashville were distributed in the counties around, each could find an ample field near his home; ·he could preach all the time and still be much with his. family. If he would maintain the character for uprightness and kindness that a preacher should in old age, he will be loved and honored as a father by his children in the faith. Brethren Grant, Logue, and Gillentine are all good preachers, and I hope the Christians within reach of Bridgeport will heartily cooperate with them in preaching the gospel in the country around. D. L.[31]

This article gave a good summary of the Rocky Springs church, almost from its beginning and even the years at Antioch.

Not much was reported after Lipscomb's and Anderson's visit in 1902 until our target date of 1914. Only a few short reports could be found in the *Gospel Advocate*. This supports what Lipscomb had said of the Rocky Springs church when he and Anderson visited in 1902—

The church, like most country churches, while maintaining the worship, has never been self-sacrificing and aggressive in spreading the gospel, as churches should be but promises to do better in the future.[32]

It appears the church was in a struggling mode at this time. We shall look at the last few reports. We have a look into an ordinary day in the existence of Rocky Springs church:

In the fall of 1906, while teaching here in Alatennga College. Brother Claus and his wife and I went out to Rocky Springs one Sunday morning when Brother Claus told the "old, old story" in his own noble way, After the sermon Elsie Arendale made the confession and a few days later she was buried with

Christ in baptism by Brother Claus. Since then, I had been inti-
mately associated with Elsie, and I always found her pure, true,
sweet, modest, kind-hearted-a faithful follower of Jesus. Elsie
was a beautiful girl about twenty-three or twenty-four years
old. It is heart-rending to her mother, I know, for it has only
been about two years since her husband died; and Irene a
younger sister, died in 1915. But God has called her higher, and
we must bow in humble submission to his will. Miss Mattie
Holder.[33]

This report was taken from the obituary of Miss Elsie Arendale. But our focus was not on the death of Miss Arendale; but
rather the weekly life of a country church, such as Rocky Springs.

Six years after the Anderson-Lipscomb visit we find the next
report. One of the large family Sewell preachers came to Rocky
Springs for a meeting. The report was as follows:

Brother W. A. Sewell's meeting at Rocky Springs, Jackson
County, Ala., closed on Tuesday evening, September 22, with
six baptisms. He is now engaged in a meeting at Dickson, Tenn.
[34]

The number of conversions was getting smaller as time
passed. This could possibly be because the Bridgeport congregation had been established and the spotlight was now on Bridgeport and not so much on Rocky Springs.

In July Charles Holder came to Rocky Springs and preached
on the third Sunday in July. His reported as follows:

South Pittsburg, July 29. 1 preached at Rocky Springs, Ala., on
the third Sunday in this month, morning, and afternoon, to
large and attentive audiences. There was one confession and
baptism. I am to hold a protracted meeting there, beginning on.
the third Sunday in August. I was in a meeting in Doran's Cove,
near Orme, from the third Sunday to the fourth Sunday night in

this month. Five were baptized. The interest and attendance were fine. Charles Holder.[35]

In August 1909 Charles Holder, who would eventually become the most popular preacher in the valley around the Bridgeport area, came to Rocky Springs and held a meeting. This meeting had better results than recent meetings. Holder's meeting was reported by S. V. Geer:

Orme, October 6.—Brother Charles Holder began a meeting at Rocky Springs, Ala., on the third Sunday in August and continued it for two weeks, closing with twenty-one baptized, one from the Baptists, and four restored. S. V. Geer.[36]

Twenty-one baptisms were the best results in a meeting at Rocky Springs since August 1896. Holder proved himself as a very effective preacher.

In 1912 the church at Rocky Springs, Ala., sent $10.25 to aid in buying property and helping build a house of worship in New Orleans.[37] This shows that the congregation was interested in other areas and their success in spreading the gospel throughout all the world.

We turn to an obituary for our next information concerning Rocky Springs. Brother Joel B. Arendale was a loyal servant of the Lord at Rocky Springs and contributed much to the church there. We see the legacy of this good man:

Early on January 19, 1914, Brother Joel B. Arendale departed from his home, near Bridgeport, Ala., for "the city which hath the foundations, whose builder and maker is God." He departed over the narrow way and will soon safely reach the city and enter through its gates into the rest prepared for the pure, true, and good. Brother Arendale was born on November 13, 1848; and while a young man he entered the church of the Lord and was a faithful member till the time of his departure. For many years he was an elder in the Rocky Springs congregation. He was true and faithful in the discharge of his duty as an elder. He was an earnest friend and persistent advocate of home and foreign missions and tried· to keep this matter before the church. God grant that we may have more such elders. Brother Arendale was a good man in every relation of life-as husband, father, brother, friend, neighbor, and citizen. We will miss him. He leaves a wife and nine children, all members of the body of Christ but one little girl not yet old enough to enter the church. His body was laid to rest at Rocky Springs, near where he had worked and worshipped for many years. Services were conducted by Brother R. W. Jernigan and the writer. Charles Holder.[38]

We give the next report even though it was published in 1915. It is given for the insight into a particular member's life at Rocky Springs. We see the best of a church's daily and annual existence through the lives of its members, as with this dear sister. R. W. Jernigan wrote the following description of Sister Sarah Johnson:

"Aunt" Sarah Johnson, of Bridgeport, Ala., went to her reward on September 1, 1915, at the age of seventy-nine years. Her husband departed this life eight years before. Sister Johnson was the mother of eleven children, seven of which are still living, all members of the church of Christ. She was the grandmother of thirty-nine children, the great-grandmother of nineteen. She was a member of the church at Rocky Springs for sixty-two years. She was blind the last twelve years of her life, but always bore her affliction with cheerfulness. A genial disposition, an exemplary life, and a devoted Christian is missed by her many friends and brethren. I visited her home frequently, and never left her fireside without feeling that I was a better man by having been in her presence. I conducted her funeral before a large crowd, and many that knew her spoke to me about her many virtues and good traits of character. R. W. Jernigan.[39]

With this report, we end the history of Rocky Springs within our parameters of time—1914. No other congregation in Jackson County has had such an interesting history from the beginning of its existence as Rocky Springs. We continue with the other congregations throughout Jackson County, Alabama. Some would be established and thrive for a while and then fade into history. Others would endure the challenges of time.

CROW CREEK

B. F. Hall came to a meeting at Crow Creek in 1826 and preached some sermons. He wrote the following interesting incident that occurred at the Crow Creek meeting:

The next meeting that I attended, as I now remember, was on Crow Creek, among the hills bordering on the line between Tennessee and Alabama. I delivered a discourse on Romans 10:1-10, in which I presented the elements of the gospel—its facts, commands and promises, and urged immediate compliance with its provisions in order to remission of sins. I invited persons forward to confess with their lips what in their hearts they believed. Several came, and among them was a venerable gentleman with a good face and fine broad, high-retreating forehead. He arose almost instantly the invitation was given. He supported with a cane his tottering frame, bent under the weight of many years, and stepped forward, and reached me his bony hand, the tears coursing down his furrowed cheeks. At the conclusion of the song, he asked if he might be permitted to say a few words. He was told to speak on. He arose, and standing nearly half-bent, supported by his cane spoke to the following effect: "Friends, I have asked permission to say a few words. You see I am an old man. I am upwards of seventy years of age. From my youth, I have been anxious to be a Christian. I have always attended religious meetings, and listened attentively to the preaching, anxious to learn what I must do to be saved. When I heard of this meeting, my first impulse was to attend it. But then I thought of my age and infirmity, and the distance, about seventy miles, and I remembered that I had never heard anything that I could understand that I must do to be saved, and it was not likely I would be more fortunate, should I come to this meeting, and I almost abandoned the idea of making the attempt. Then again, I remembered my great age and declining life, and knew I could not live much longer, and the thought of dying without religion was horrible. These reflections armed me with resolution to undertake the long and fatiguing journey, with the faint hope that maybe, I shall hear something that will give me hope and comfort in death. I devoutly thank God that I am here, and that I have been permitted to hear the sermon today. It is the first time in life that I have heard, so that I could understand, what I must do to become a Christian. Young friends, if I had, when I was of your age, heard the discourse to which you have just listened, I would have then become a Christian." At this sad story of the poor old man many wept, and no wonder, it was enough to move a heart of stone.

We heard the confession of the weeping penitents, and instantly repaired to the water but a few paces from the stand, when they were all immersed into Christ Jesus. As the old gentleman emerged from the liquid grave a smile played over his features, blending with his tears; he clapped together his thin hands, and said, "Thanks be to God for the assurance I now feel that my sins are forgiven! I have believed his word, and, as I trust, have from the heart complied with his prescribed conditions of pardon, and, confiding in his word of promise, I rejoice to be assured of my acceptance with my adorable Savior. I can now return home contented and happy and occupy the few remaining days I may yet live on earth in making ready for the life to come. Friends, one and all, farewell. Our next meeting will be at the judgment. May I hope to see you all in heaven?" At this affecting talk of the old man many wept. It was the last day of the meeting. The congregation soon dispersed. I assisted the old man on his horse, and bade him a final adieu, and never heard of him afterwards, but hope to meet him in heaven. O what meetings and greetings, and joyful recognitions there will be in the spirit world![40]

The Crow Creek mentioned by Hall was approximately sixteen or seventeen miles northwest of Rocky Springs, near the Tennessee-Alabama state line. The meeting that Hall attended at Crow Creek reveals that meetings had been occurring there prior to this meeting. This work could possibly be the second work established in Jackson County, Alabama.

Crow Creek's next mentioned related to the community as just a point on the railroad:

> Every employee of the N.& C. R. R as well as every Christian brother who has been to Cowan Bro. Rufe Sartain, the one-legged engineer. He has been in the employment of the company longer than any other engineer connected with the road. He is master of his trade, few men knowing more about the intricate machinery of a locomotive than he. During a meeting at Cowan last year, I took a trip with him on his engine through the tunnel over to Crow Creek and back.[41]

As one can see the only thing verified in this report is that in 1889 Crow Creek was still a community. Nothing about the church was mentioned. The congregation was still around. By 1895 reports began to trickle into the *Gospel Advocate*. E. H. Boyd and Charles Holder were the main preachers during the 1890's.

Crow Creek was not very vivacious, apparently, because the next mention in the records was not 1895. Boyd sends the first report. He mentions all his preaching points:

Jasper, March 6.... I am preaching once a month at the following points: Tracy City, Rocky Springs, Ala., Bridgeport, Ala., Crow Creek, Ala., and Bethel, Tenn. At all of these points I find more than usual interest manifested and a more effectual working in the measure or every part of the body, which makes the outlook for the future of these churches hopeful for additions and growth in grace as well. Brethren pray for me, for verily the fields are white unto harvest, and the laborers few. E. H. Boyd.[42]

Maybe some life was coming back into Crow Creek; as Boyd said of all his preaching points—... "which make the outlook for the future of these churches hopeful for additions and growth in grace as well." That sounds good for Crow Creek.

In 1896 J. H. Morton reported that Boyd had preached at Crow Creek. His report was really about Bridgeport, but the Crow Creek reference was incidental and gave more insight into the Crow Creek work. The report stated:

Brother E. H. Boyd, of Jasper, Tenn., stopped a few hours at Bridgeport, on his return from Crow Creek, his regular appointment. One was baptized by him there. Brother Boyd is an old-fashioned gospel preacher. He has been in feeble health for some time. but we are glad to report that he is now improving. The Lord bless the faithful in Christ everywhere! J. H. Morton.[43]

Morton gave us a look at Boyd's health condition also. He was, however, on the mend. This report was the last report to appear in the *Gospel Advocate*, concerning Crow Creek. What became to this congregation is unknown to the writer.

SAUTA CAVE

When Jackson County was created in 1819, Sauta Cave was established as the temporary seat of justice, but shortly thereafter it was moved to the village of Sauta located near Birdsong Spring. In 1828, county records were moved into the new brick, two-story courthouse in Bellefonte which served as the county seat for 40 years.

The earliest reference to any kind of activity among our brethren at Sauta Cave came from Washington Bacon. This was in 1867, which makes us wonder if the congregation had its beginning before the Civil War. Let us take a close look at the report:

> Trenton, GA., Aug. 19, 1867. Bros. Fanning and Lipscomb: I left home on Friday before the first Lord's day, last, for Rocky Springs, Jackson county, Ala. I preached for the brethren on Saturday and Lord's day, and set in order the things that were wanting, and closed with one addition: left to go to Sorta (Sauta) Cave, in the same county, arrived there on Thursday, preached to a few of the brethren at night, continued the meeting until Monday, set the congregation in order, and closed with eight additions – two from the Methodists, one from the

Baptists: and five from the world. I then turned my course homeward, tarried all night, with Bro. Mitchell, he preached next day and the night following at his house, continued my speech from candle lighting until 11 o'clock at night; I then gave an invitation, and two persons came forward —Bro. Q. J. Mitchell's wife and her aged mother, sixty-seven years old. This made in all eleven accessions to the army of the saints, during this short tour. In hope of eternal life, Washington Bacon.[44]

We learn that Bacon set the congregation in order, which suggests that the congregation had matured enough to be organized. When our pioneer preachers speak of organizing a congregation, they mean that they appointed elders and deacons. That does not happen until the Christians have matured enough to become leaders. The next report also came from Washington Bacon. It was published in December 1869. He wrote:

At Sota (Sauta) Cave, embracing the first Lord's Day inst., there was one addition making in all, thirty additions at protracted meetings. At my other meetings I have not noticed the numbers, perhaps they would swell the number to forty in all. To the good Lord be all the glory, Amen and amen. May grace, peace, and mercy be with all those that love our Lord Jesus Christ with pure heart fervently. Amen. Your loving brother, Washington Bacon.[45]

By now you will have realized that either Bacon or a printer for the *Gospel Advocate* had difficulty in spelling "Sauta." This congregation had been planted by someone whose name is lost in time.

In 1874 Joseph Wheeler visited the Sauta congregation and held a meeting. Wheeler described it:

Brethren L. &: S: I have been preaching as I had opportunity this year, the result is as follows: At Kennamer Cove three have made the good confession and were baptized. Many others fully convinced that God's decrees do not cause the people to act as they do and are almost persuaded to be Christians. Eleven have been baptized here at Sorta (Sauta) congregation. Others would be if it were not for "father and mother."[46]

Our next report came in 1883. Even this report had misspelled "Sauta" as "Santa." It was written by Dr. D. M. Breaker of Chattanooga, Tennessee. He wrote of the small group at Sauta Cave:

Editors Gospel Advocate: I held a four days' meeting in Santa (Sauta) Valley, Ala., last week. It had been arranged to use the Methodist house of worship, but someone told the trustees that I was "a talented man and would tear their church all to pieces," and they withdrew their permission. Bro. W. C. Stephens, an excellent man and a devoted Christian, by the way, was not to be outdone; and so, he cleaned out his workshop, and arranged it for preaching. The meeting was a very interesting one. I had the pleasure of baptizing a beautiful and intelligent young lady, a daughter of Bro. Stephens. D. M. Breaker.[47]

We feel compelled to give the following information on Dr. Breaker:

At the close of the revival services at the Christian church, Chattanooga, Wednesday evening last, Dr. D. M. Breaker, a Baptist minister of high character, excellent abilities and well and favorably known in the South, presented himself for membership, and read to the congregation a statement, in which he set forth his reasons for leaving the Baptist church and uniting himself with the Christian. Nashville Banner, September 1st. Reprinted by the Gospel Advocate.[48]

Just over a month later David Lipscomb was defending him

from angry and slanderous remarks made by Breaker's former Baptist brethren. Lipscomb wrote:

> Elder D. M. Breaker has for years been an active and somewhat prominent member of the Baptist church. He recently united with the disciples at Chattanooga. During the time of his membership in the Baptist church, not a word against him '".as published. When he united with the disciples, although he spoke not an unkind word, as we learn, concerning his former brethren, the Baptist paper published at Chattanooga slurs his character. We say this, regardless of what Breaker's character may have been, of which we have no specific knowledge. But to fellowship a man for years, make no charges against him so long as he remains with our party, then, when he voluntarily leaves it, to injure him by insinuation and inuendo, is sectarian meanness, or mean sectarianism, wherever found. If a man is guilty of a wrong that makes it proper to expose him, the only fair and manly way is to tell what his crimes are. The man that insinuates something is wrong with a man and does not state it in such a way that he can meet it, is the assassin of character. If there was anything wrong with Elder Breaker's character, why did you not deal with him and expose him when in the Baptist church. All thinking men will believe the slur at his character is not because he is unworthy, but because he left. their party. D. L.[49]

Breaker began preaching among churches of Christ almost immediately after uniting with the Chattanooga congregation. He came to Sauta Cave within five months after becoming a member of the church.

In 1885 a young man by the name of Jones came to Sauta and preached. He made quite an impression upon the members at that place and W. C. Stephens wrote about the meeting and young Jones:

Dear Brethren Lipscomb and Sewell: I am requested to make a report of a meeting held with the above congregation by a. 17-year-old boy, by the name of Jones of Madison county, Ala. The meeting was on the Lord's day, which was the first Lord's day in June. The theme of his discourse at eleven o'clock was "Faith and Works. The subject was Ephesians 2:8. He preached for one hour and fifteen minutes. At the close he gave an invitation; two came forward and were baptized the same day. He preached again at night. His discourse was as good as I ever heard. He preached one hour and twenty minutes, and at the close gave an invitation and one came forward demanding baptism and was baptized the same hour of the night. The cause of our Lord and Master is progressing in this country. Bro Jones in his youth needs encouragement; he is going to make a man at the head of the list of the reformation if he has the proper encouragement. I have known his father from youth; he is a very worthy man. They are both from the Missionary Baptists, less than twelve months ago. Bro. B. C. Goodwin preached here Wednesday night, the night of our regular prayer meeting. His discourse was on practical Christianity. At the close he gave an invitation; one noble young lady came forward and made the good confession. At the baptism this morning, be made a. short talk on the design of baptism. One came forward and was baptized; at the same time, a member of the Baptists of forty years good standing, united with us on the Bible. The whole congregation rejoiced and gave God, our Father, the praise. The church throughout North Ala., as far as I hear, is in a prosperous condition.

Our preaching brethren seem to be more in earnest than ever before. The elders and deacons and lay members seem to be fully aroused to their duty. Sectarianism is giving way to the truth. Our protracted meeting comes off the third Lord's day in August. W. C. Stephens.[50]

Instead of praising the work at Sauta, Lipscomb rants about giving too much praise to a young preacher. I do not know if

Lipscomb had an "ax to grind" with W. C. Stephens or the rural Jackson County churches in general, but something seemed to be "stuck in his craw." His comment was:

> If our young brother can stand such hurtful puffing as the above without ruin, he is better than ordinary. It is strange brethren cannot give judicious encouragement to young brethren, without such hurtful flattery as the above.[51]

Like so many other congregations Sauta Cave faded into time. We do not know when this work ceased, but 1885 was the last year any report came forth from the *Gospel Advocate*. That is a good sign that the work ended soon afterward—maybe a few months or maybe a year or so.

DRY COVE

Dry Cove lies about seven and a half miles southwest of Scottsboro. It is located about four miles southeast of Sauta Cave. This quiet little community drew Joseph Wheeler from Trenton, Georgia sometime between September 1867 and December 1873. He located there and began preaching in the community and established a preaching circuit throughout the area. His first report is given as it was published in the *Gospel Advocate*:

> Bro. Joseph Wheeler, writes from Dry Cove, Alabama, that he has recently baptized four persons where he has been laboring but did not name the point where they were baptized.[52]

It seems that Wheeler had collected a small group to worship as the New Testament directs. A short report from W. C. Stephens was published and it read: "We have a small band of disciples at this place who meet nearly every Lord's day to break bread."[53]

W. C. Stephens seemed to be everywhere—he was at Dry Cove in 1875. We find him at Sauta Cave in 1882 and Larkinsville when it began in 1886. Did he have "wanderlust" and had to keep moving? He was a land speculator, owned and operated a cotton gin, and became a medical doctor. He had talent and was quite knowledgeable in the Bible. He spent the last thirty years of his life in Bagwell, Texas where he died on April 26, 1923.[54] He made contributions in various ways to the struggling churches in the south end of Jackson County.

The next report was given by Joseph Wheeler. He gave information about a father refusing to allow her to be baptized. He stated:

> Brethren L. &: S: I have been preaching as I had opportunity this year, the result is as follows: At Kennamer Cove three have made the good confession and were baptized. Many others fully convinced that God's decrees do not cause the people to act as they do and are almost persuaded to be Christians. Eleven have been baptized here at Sorta congregation. Others would be if it were not for "father and mother." Joseph Wheeler. Dry Cove, Jackson Co., Ala. Nov. 10th, 1874.[55]

A young Christian from Dry Cove, J. H. Gregory, was advertising in the *Gospel Advocate* for a teaching position somewhere. He had standards that had to be met. The *Gospel Advocate* stated: "He is a young man without family and will accept no position unless in the neighborhood of a congregation of disciples.[56] Gregory was to be commended for having such requirements before he would accept a teaching position somewhere.

In October 1875 W. C. Stephens writes:

> We have a small band of disciples at this place who meet nearly every Lord's day to break bread. We have the services of Bro. Jos. Wheeler once a month. He is a faithful warrior in the Lord's vineyard.[57]

David Lipscomb wrote in the *Gospel Advocate* concerning Joseph Wheeler:

Bro. Joe Wheeler, of Dry Cove, Ala., is doing a good work in a much-neglected portion of the Lord's vineyard. He recently had a debate with one Warren, a Hard-shell Baptist1 in which the latter brought forward his convincing proof, that baptism for remission of sins was unnecessary, the statement that his mother had died without being baptized, because she felt unworthy, and that she had gone to heaven for he had seen her since she went there. No doubt, Mr. Warren is what school boys would call "a good 'un."[58]

Wheeler was getting ready to move to another location and establish a new preaching circuit. When he relocated it was published in the *Gospel Advocate*. He relocated to Bridgeport.[59]

J. M. Gainer gave what may have been the last report on Dry Cove. It was published in September 1912. He wrote an inclusive statement; but very short and said "... interesting meetings at Boaz and Dry Cove."[60] That was the last mention of Dry Cove in the *Gospel Advocate*. No other records have been revealed to date (2024).

Joseph Wheeler and his mentor—Washington Bacon kept the church from the end of the Civil War to the mid-1880s. The churches in the northeastern part of the state owe a great debt of gratitude to these two men. Dry Cove may never have been if Joseph Wheeler had never set foot in that region of Jackson County. We see that within a few years after he moves to the Bridgeport area the church sinks into the black hole of the forgotten.

LARKINSVILLE

Larkinsville is a historic village and populated place in Jackson County, Alabama, United States. It lies two miles west of Scottsboro, Alabama. Founded in 1828 by David Larkin, it was incorporated into the nearby city of Scottsboro in the late 1960s. In 1895, Larkinsville had a population of 216. As late as 1940, the population was 320 according to the U.S. Census in Alabama.

Our first knowledge of a church at Larkinsville came to us from the pen of V. M. Metcalfe. The note was:

> At Larkinsville I met Bro. W. C. Stephens, who lives in the country, some six miles, went home with him, and spoke Monday night to a good crowd of his neighbors. We have no fine house in which to worship at this place; yet Bro. Stephens had swept out his blacksmith shop, and put up a good stove, and made it quite comfortable. Bro. Stephens and his neighbors, a few brethren among them, are trying and expect soon to have a good house of worship ready; so, when any of our brethren pass that way, they can have a house in which to preach. You will meet a faithful little band of disciples. V. M. Metcalfe.[61]

The next report came through a question written to John T. Poe of Texas. It was written by T. S. Stephens. He made the following inquiry:

> Dear Bro. Poe: I have seen some very interesting questions in your Bible Class, which have caused me to search the Bible a great deal, and in searching, I found some questions which I wish to ask. Who of the twelve tribes of Israel dipped his foot in oil and wore iron and brass shoes, and who was the fat king? As this is my first to write to any paper, I will close for fear I say too much. T. S. Stephens, Larkinsville, Ala., January 31st, 1884.[62]

B. C. Goodwin came and preached on April 26, 1885. He reported three confessions and baptisms on that day.[63] Just when a congregation had been planted at this time is not clear. But the next report just over a year later helps give the desired answer:

> Bro. W. T. (C.) Stephens from Larkinsville writes: "Three years ago, there were but few disciples in this country. What preaching we had was done in my work shop and in private houses. Bro. J. W. (H.) Morris preached for us in 1883 and did much good. Bro. B. C. Goodman (Goodwin) preached here last year, has moved here and is a good worker both on the farm and in the pulpit. He preaches 1st Lord's day at Rocky Springs, 2nd. at Paint Rock Station; 3rd at home, 4tb at Kennamer's Cove and 5th in some destitute neighborhood. At his last meeting here, three made the good confession. We meet every Lord's day to worship. We invite all to read and study the Bible with us. We have 17 members in good working order."[64]

Notice that Stephens said that "Three years ago, there were but few disciples in this country." And that preaching was done either in private houses or in his workshop. This suggests that there was a cell group in Larkinsville as early as 1882. The report also said that B. C. Goodwin had moved into the community and was preaching at Larkinsville as a part of his preaching circuit.

O. P. Spiegel came to Larkinsville and preached an eight-day meeting in the early part of May 1886. W. C. Stephens wrote a full report of this meeting:

> W. C. Stephens, of Zion's Rest, near Larkinsville, writes May 19th, 1886: "It has been some time since you were bothered with a report from us. I wish to report a meeting conducted by one of Bro. Larimore's students, a young man of twenty years, by the name of O. P. Speegal (sic). He began on Friday night before the second Lord's day in May and continued until the Friday night following. He preached nine discourses and handled the old Jerusalem blade well for a boy. He will stand in the class at or near the head in a few years if he goes on to school a while longer, which I hope he will. The immediate result of the meeting is that a man and his wife came to Bro. Goodwin on the third Lord's day morning and told him that they were convinced and demanded baptism at his hands. So, the husband and wife were united together in the church of the first born. The good work is still moving on here. May God our Father bless Bro. Larimore in laborers into the vineyard of our Master, to whom we give all the glory."[65]

As is the case many times—the devil seems to show up at an inconvenient time. This struggling congregation had a huge problem to develop. It nearly destroyed the work at Larkinsville. The *Gospel Advocate* eventually published both sides of the event as told by the persons involved. The following excerpt will give the reader a vivid picture as to how the problem developed:

> A brother from Larkinsville, Ala., gives us a case in which the relatives of an elder in the church misbehaved at church, so as to disturb the audience, This brother took out a warrant for these

disturbers of the worship, and on account of this the elder and his family have ceased to attend church. This brother wishes to know if he did right. If it is right for the church to punish men and women through civil authority for interfering with religious worship —for persecuting them or committing offenses against the cause of God, it was right to do it to these persons, provided they had been remonstrated with, and milder means used to induce them to desist. No Christian is justified in using harsh and severe measures to affect an object until mild ones have failed. A man who resorts to harsh and extreme measures on slight provocations never will have much more weight in a community. He will be regarded as harsh, vengeful and bitter in his feelings. A man that is ready to run to the church with every little difficulty instead of patiently trying to settle them in the way that would be least offensive to the parties who did the wrong, fails in an essential Christian element. So, a man who inflicts the punishments of the law, when it can be possibly avoided, will never be regarded as a patient, kind, long-suffering, forbearing man. These are the elements of a Christian character that ought; to be presented to the world. Without them a man can have but little weight as a Christian. Admitting that it is right for Christians to prosecute men with the civil power, we — could not answer whether this brother did right or not, until we knew whether he had exhausted mild and gentle means to stop the evil. If he had done this, on the supposition that it is right for the Christian to prosecute the disturber of their worship, he was justified in what he did. But kindness is the spirit of Christianity that works effectually.[66]

The problem seemed to be a "Diotrephesian" problem—one man casting people out of the church or forbidding them to come back. There was no evidence that this man was an elder or even a deacon. We do not have information as to whether he consulted with elders or not before he took such drastic measures. From the response to the above article, it seems that he acted on his own.

We do not know his name—he signed the report simply a brother. [67] David Lipscomb wrote:

> But I doubt whether Christians should ever prosecute those who persecute them. Disturbing worship is a kind of persecution. They ought to return good for evil and overcome evil with good. That is the Christian law. D.L.[68]

The response to this report was written to Lipscomb by a Brother Levi Kennamer. His side of the story was a personal one, and it shed more light on the incident and helped to give a better sense of what really happened at Larkinsville. The *Gospel Advocate* read as follows:

> Bro. Lipscomb: I see in the Gospel Advocate No. 38, present volume, a question asked by a brother from Larkinsville, to know if he had done right in prosecuting some disturber of public worship, and that an elder of the church and his family have absented themselves on account of the disturbers being relatives of his.
>
> If the statement in the interrogatory had been correct your reply would not have been so objection able, and as I am the elder referred to, and have been pretty badly "grubbed" in the reply, I claim the right to make some statements concerning the matter for myself.
>
> Two of them were distant relatives of mine, and if that is the cause of my action in the matter I ought to be ready to agree with you that I would be very narrow-minded. But I had rather state the cause for myself:
>
> "Several years ago, there was a congregation in this neighborhood, and it became destroyed by the conduct of some of its members, our Larkinsville brother being one of the number and it remained this way for several years. About three years ago the cause began to revive a little, and about two and a half years ago I went into the congregation and was chosen an elder and have

done my duty as far as I could learn it from the word, and the cause became prosperous, the people seemed to be interested, and the congregation was seventy-five strong. But, when this matter occurred, it just killed out all the influence we had gained, and I have absented myself from the congregation because there is no available good that can be done at present. Our brother is harsh, inconsiderate, uncontrollable, and will go into such things without seeing where he will get out.

Bro. Lipscomb, you seem to be in doubt whether a brother has a right to take out a warrant or not. The spirit of God commands us to be subject to the powers that be, but nowhere to make ourselves part of that power. Rom. viii: 9, "Now if any man have not the spirit of Christ, he is none of his." Now if we can find where Christ, in his personal ministry, commanded it, or where the comforter that he sent into the world directed it, we can use it; if not, we ought to let it alone.

If you can see any advice to me in this, it will be gladly received. I think justice to myself, and the cause in this county, and especially to the readers of the Advocate, would demand a publication of this. Your Brother, Levi Kennamer.[69]

Lipscomb answers in a stern tone and we give his entire response:

We answer the queries as propounded; so, our brother does not differ with us in what we said. We knew them only as given us, and no names were mentioned. I have no doubt of the impropriety of calling on the civil powers to punish those who persecute and misuse us, but many believe it is right, and I cannot expect those who so believe to act according to my faith; but my aim was to show that, according to their theory, it should not be done until all mild Christian measures had failed.

We are glad to know that our brother did not cease to serve the Lord because his relatives were punished. This is so often the case that we are glad to find it is not so now. We frequently know cases where a wicked son is dealt with and the whole family is estranged and ceases to serve God. But we are sorry to learn our brother lets himself be driven from the service of God because of the imprudence and harsh measures of some weak man. He did not learn to do this from the word of God. The idea that a, church, or Christians. are justified in ceasing to meet, and worship God because some man or men do badly, or act imprudently, is contrary to all the teaching of the Bible.

Suppose Christ, whom Judas betrayed, Peter denied, and all forsook, had given up and left us as our brother leaves him. suppose because Ananias and Sapphira lied the apostles had quit, because the church at Corinth upheld one guilty of incest, and evil workers were in the church, they all had given up and quit. Paul said nothing should separate him from Christ. Our brother separates himself from Christ (to separate himself from his church, his worship, his service is to separate himself from Christ) because another brother in his weakness, his human infirmity, his lack of knowledge does wrong. Such a course will destroy the church of God anywhere. He says: ' No good can be done.' Who is it that cannot do good? God· does all the good that man receives. Cannot God do good? Does one man, sinning, disable God to do good to another striving to do his duty? Man's " sins separate between him and his God." But another's sin cannot separate between me and my God, and another' sins shall never drive me from the anctu1 1ry and mercy seat or my God.

Our brother doubtless means that the world will be driven off by the course mentioned. But does he, meet to worship God only to benefit the world? Does he need no help from God, that he can receive only waiting on God, in the appointments of God? Is he strong enough to walk without God's, help? I need to worship God because I am weak: I am frail, I am sinful, and desire to draw near to, God, that he may bless and strengthen and help me in my weakness and helplessness. I would do it if not another sinner ever attended worship, because I want God's nearness, his strength, his help. But then, such difficulties affect the world only, because the servants of God let it shame their faith, cool their zeal, paralyze their efforts, and forsake God, so that he will not work with and through them. O brethren (for I write for others who are in the same condition. of our brother) confess your sins, turn to God, wait; on him in his appointments, and be his children, that he may abundantly bless you and save you, and through you bless the world.

Certainly, the brother acted hastily and did very wrong, as I before stated, if he appealed to the civil law without kindly trying to correct the wrong. Especially was it a wrong to the young ladies who were trying to quiet the drunk men, Doubtless they were mortified at the course of their companions enough without being dragged into court, and I think the brother ought to apologize to them and to the church and community for his hastiness in doing as he did. But, if he does not, it does not justify any Christian in refusing to worship God in his appointments, and I think our brother ought to ask forgiveness of God and of his brethren for absenting himself from the services of God and go back to his place in the Sanctuary of the Lord, and God will bless us as we are fitted to receive. We think our brother's excuse for forsaking the assembling of himself with the church is no better than the one assigned by the other brother. It is all wrong to quit God's service because some poor human being does wrong. D.L.[70]

It is interesting that Lipscomb condemned both parties for not acting in the manner they should have acted. During this same time, the minister—B. C. Goodwin had asked Lipscomb a question about the Adventists in the vicinity of Larkinsville:

We are surrounded by Adventists, and they, contend that there is no principle in man that lives between death and the resurrection, and some of our best brethren are believing it, and it is exciting some controversy, and we wish an article from one or the other on this subject. We are seeking truth, and if the Bible does teach it, we want to know it, and if it does not, we want to know it; and you can settle this trouble by giving an article on it. Give us the Scriptures bearing on it. B. C. Goodwin, Larkinsville, Ala.

You must have a sorry set of brethren about Larkinsville, if they are causing trouble on this question. What has this question to do with any man's salvation? There are many truths in the world that are of no benefit to salvation. Men who can leave the practical precepts of the Christian religion, while their neighbors are in darkness, to create trouble over these foolish questions are very weak members of the church of Christ. The question has no more to do with a man's Christian life than the question what makes one horse bay another gray. There is not a sentence in the Bible that was intended to teach what man's condition between death and the resurrection is, and men who attempt to teach these things are teaching questions that gender strife to no profit. This is true not only of this question, but of almost every question presented by the Adventists there is nothing practical in anything they present as matter of faith, and they with foolish questions disturb the faith of weak men and women. D.L.[71]

It seems that Lipscomb was close to "burnout" by the quick short answers he gave Goodwin and the brethren around Larkinsville. This caused Goodwin and his brethren to lose some of their esteem toward Lipscomb and Goodwin was the kind of man who could not take that sort of treatment, so, Goodwin, a little more than five weeks later, fires back at Lipscomb trying to get a well thought out answer. It read thus:

Bro. Lipscomb, after long consideration I answer your answer concerning the doctrine taught by the Adventist in our community. Your answer was by no means satisfactory. We do not know whether you mean that we are poor in knowledge or in purse. If we are in knowledge, we agree with you and we think the way you answered the query is calculated to keep us poor in knowledge. The first objection we make to your answer is the spirit in which you answered. We look to you as children look to a father for instructions. Then as this is the case. if one of your children in your family was to draw a conclusion from meditating upon the discipline of your family which you did not intend to teach, would you as a kind father criticize him for being poor in knowledge? No, if you loved him, you would try in a kind spirit to lead him out of the wrong in which he has fallen. Then, Bro. L., we think you should have treated us in this way; Bro. L. the brethren in this country think well of you, and dote upon your paper, and the way you have treated us does not make us fall out with you. We will love you and the Advocate in spite of all your crabid (sic) answers. We agree with you in regard to there being nothing written in the Bible with the purpose to teach anything in regard to the condition of man between death and the judgment, still a passage of scripture may be written to prove one thing and prove a great many other things, if they do not conflict with the first. Then Bro. L., as it has created some unpleasant feeling, I can but wish I had not written the inquiry for we have some as good brethren here as anywhere: and they are liberal. B. C. Goodwin. Larkinsville.[72]

Lipscomb answered Goodwin still in a curt response which seemed he was more interested in the fact that Goodwin and the Larkinsville brethren were disturbed at this teaching that he was to give them an answer to their question. Keep in mind that this was after Lipscomb had read the compliments Goodwin had showered upon Lipscomb about how much the brethren looked up to him as children looked up to their father. Lipscomb wrote his response:

Bro. G. owns that no Scripture was written for the purpose of teaching the condition of the dead between death and the resurrection. It is only incidentally taught. Christ and the Holy Spirit purposed to teach everything necessary to life and godliness. If they did not purposely teach something on this subject it was because nothing coercing this, is unnecessary to life nod godliness. There are many things incidentally taught that it would be a crime to introduce into the teaching of the church as a part of the faith. Again, we ought to purpose to teach exactly what the Savior and the Spirit purposed to teach. It is a crime to purpose, to add a single thing of our teaching to that he purposed to teach. It is a purposed crime against God to teach something he never purposed to teach.

Then with considerable opportunity for observing. I have never known a single instance of a church or individual that began to agitate these questions that did not lose all interest the Christian religion and lose their influence for good. I have known good men that held opinions both ways, which maintained their zeal and earnestness as Christians, but they did not preach it, or agitate it publicly or privately. It then seems to me akin to treason to the Christ and his cause, to introduce questions concerning which, he never purposely taught anything, and which so destroys the life of his people. And we are glad that we have love enough for Christ and his Church to feel indignation whenever these questions are introduced to divide his people and destroy spiritual life in his children. Especially it is very wrong to a community where the truth and church of God are weak and are struggling for existence and the people are going down to ruin, because the vital truths of the gospel have not taught them, to introduce strife among them on such queries.[73]

1886 was not a very good year for Larkinsville—too much controversy —both internally and externally.

It seems that at some point in the late 1890s the Larkinsville work ceased to exist. But in 1944 another work began at Larkinsville. W. R. Craig of Scottsboro reported:

W. R. Craig, Box 255, Scottsboro, Ala., March 6: "The small congregation at Larkinsville, in this county, has purchased from the Church of God people a very desirable meetinghouse. There are only five men in this little church, and they are going to need some outside help to pay for the building. The church in Scottsboro is contributing $100 toward the purchase price of this building and is asking others to have fellowship with it in this good work. If you would have part in this work, send your contribution to Bill Stewart, Larkinsville, Ala.[74]

In this report it is stated that the tiny congregation had purchased a "desirable meetinghouse" from the Church of God. They were struggling so much that the only way they could purchase the building was to secure help.

A well-known preacher in North Alabama was Jack Wilhelm, who grew up in this region. He preached his first sermon here in 1945.[75] Another well-known preacher from this area was Charles Cobb. Cobb's final work was with the Larkinsville Church of Christ, where he worked for 17 years. Cobb died on July 8, 2004.[76]

The reason that the work of the original congregation at Larkinsville ended is not clear. We glean a statement concerning the Larkinsville church that may give a clue as to what really caused the death of the earlier work. It was taken from Levi Kennamer's report of November 10, 1886. The statement was:

> Several years ago, there was a congregation in this neighborhood, and it became destroyed by the conduct of some of its members, our Larkinsville brother being one of the number, and it remained this way for several years.[77]

It would be speculation on our part to say that the above-mentioned incident was the reason the work ended, but it is to be considered. Perhaps many obstacles, maybe too many obstacles to overcome were the cause.

This ends our history of the Larkinsville congregation. The history of this congregation demonstrates how quickly a work can be established and then disappear. It began with so much promise and then faded into oblivion. We need to be ever mindful that we must strive to not have strife in our churches, but peace and harmony.

Bridgeport

The Nashville, Chattanooga, and St. Louis Railway and the Memphis and Charleston Railroad cross the Tennessee River at Bridgeport. Here, also, the river crosses, or cuts through, the mountain range that passes through Tennessee into Alabama.

Some years ago, some promoters and capitalists selected this point to build a large city. They graded streets on a magnificent scale, built fine business houses and a number of dwellings and factories, brought water from a mountain spring, and put in an electric plant to supply lights for a city with thirty thousand people. The city failed to materialize; so, there are a number of large and costly buildings that can be bought cheap-some of them unfinished and going to wreck. It is a good shipping point for mining and manufacturing and may yet grow to a place of importance.

Like most congregations in this area, the Bridgeport church of Christ had its roots in the Rocky Springs Church which began in that community in the early eighteen hundreds. By 1893, there were enough brethren in Bridgeport who wanted their own meeting place, following a ten-day meeting in which F. D. Srygley did the preaching, the church met regularly. The first service of this meeting was April 9. 1893. On November 4, 1894, the following men were appointed elders: W. L. McFarlane, C. W. C. Hall, and G. T. Rutledge. The deacons were R. D. Vaughn, H. L. Taylor, and G. W. Fennamore, W. L. McFarlane was the treasurer. [78]

An interesting note—J. H. Morton caught a train to Bridgeport and got off at the station, but apparently his intentions were not to preach at Bridgeport. He wrote:

> Bridgeport, Aug; 27. On Friday, Aug. 14, we left our home (near Berlin, Tenn.), and boarded a train for Bridgeport, Ala. Arriving at Bridgeport, we were met at the train by Brother J. R. Johnson, who furnished us conveyance to his home, near Rocky Spring Church. We commenced our meeting at Rocky Spring on Saturday night, August 16, and continued the meeting' ten days, resulting in twenty-four additions from an sources. The meeting" closed with a good interest. Two confessed the Savior on the last night of the meeting. We had promised only eighteen days' preaching in Jackson County. Ala. Doran's Cove claimed the balance of our time.[79]

The interesting thing about this trip is that Bridgeport was not mentioned at that time in Morton's list of preaching points in Jackson County, even though the congregation had just been established by F. D. Srygley in April. Had he planned his tour before Bridgeport had been established? We do not know. It is interesting that Bridgeport was left out of his list of appointments; but in his next report on this trip, he tells us that he had extended his tour so he could hold a gospel meeting at Bridgeport. Did Brother Johnson, who lived near the new congregation at Bridgeport, persuade him to also preach at Bridgeport? Something changed his mind as we see in this next report:

> Bridgeport, Sept. 11.—We are still preaching the old Jerusalem gospel in Jackson County, Ala., preaching now in the Presbyterian house of worship in Bridgeport. One young lady

confessed the Savior last night, and we expect to baptize her in the Tennessee River today. We had intended to leave for our home (Berlin, Tenn.) today. This is the longest time we have been away from our dear motherless children since their mother (our own dear Maggie) crossed over the river. I received a letter from home today, from the children, and they write: "Papa, don't be uneasy about us; we are all well and doing well. Stay as long as you can accomplish good; the Lord will provide. for us." I will remain here a few days longer. There have been seventy-six enlisted under our great King in my meetings during the past Eleven weeks. Praise the Lord! I pray my Heavenly Father, if it be consistent with his will, to spare my life to see four thousand more enlist under Jesus, the Captain of our salvation. My cup of joy will be full if it be the Lord's will that I shall have been the humble agent in the Lord's army of holding up Jesus to a perishing world until eight thousand shall have enlisted in the army of Christ. Brother S. M. Cook, missionary to West Africa, has been with us several days in our meetings at Doran's Cove and Bridgeport, and he has given us much valuable assistance in our song and prayer service. I wish him every success in his work across the sea. Brother E. H. Boyd, of Jasper, Tenn., stopped a few hours at Bridgeport, on his return from Crow Creek, his regular appointment. One was baptized by him there. Brother Boyd is an old-fashioned gospel preacher. He has been in feeble health for some time. but we are glad to report that he Is now improving. The Lord bless the faithful in Christ everywhere! J. H. Morton.[80]

It can readily be seen that the extended time at Bridgeport paid off with a young lady coming to Christ. Any time just one soul is added to the Lord's Kingdom it is a success.

In 1902 the church, with the aid of surrounding congregations, opened a school to train preachers at Bridgeport. The following excerpt was taken from "In And Around Bridgeport:"

In 1902 the Alatennga College was opened with J. W. Grant as President; Professor A. B. Blazer as Vice President and Secretary; and the following faculty: Miss Aida Cambron, B. A.; Honorable J. S. Benson; Miss Canna Wynne; Miss Lula Burger; Miss Ollie V. Hughes and Miss Mattie Holder. The school was located in a new four-story sandstone building that was built on the corner of Alabama Avenue and Eighth Street. The course of study was included in five departments: Collegiate, Intermediate, Preparatory, Commercial, and Primary. Optional courses were offered in Bible, Art, Elocution and Music. The college closed about 1908 when Alatennga sold its property to the Southern Baptist Association.[81]

The next report on the work at Bridgeport came seven years later. Charles Holder came and held a meeting beginning on the fifth Sunday night and continued until the fourth Sunday night in September. S. V. Geer gave a good report on this meeting:

Orme, October 6. Brother Charles Holder began a meeting at Rocky Springs, Ala., on the third Sunday in August and continued it two weeks, closing with twenty-one baptized, one from the Baptists, and four restored. From there he went to Bridgeport, Ala., where he began a meeting on the fifth Sunday night in August. (He) Continued till the fourth Sunday night in September, and closing with seventeen baptized, one from the Baptists, on from the Methodists, and two restored.[82]

This meeting was a great success for the still-infant Bridgeport church. It would grow to become a great light in that part of the valley. It would overshadow the Rocky Springs work in a few years. The next report was written by Charles Holder, who was worshipping regularly with the Bridgeport congregation. He wrote:

Bridgeport. Ala., November 5. Brother W. T. Boaz, of Columbia, Tenn., was with my home congregation here at Bridgeport from the third to the fourth Sunday in September in a fine meeting. We had large crowds and fine attention at every service. Interest fine, preaching fine, and great good done. Seven were baptized and the church was much strengthened. Brother Boaz is to be with us again next year. The churches at Bridgeport and Scottsboro, Ala., are to use Brother R. W. Jernigan in evangelizing Jackson County, Ala., next year. Brother Jernigan recently gave up school-teaching and located at Bridgeport to do the work of an evangelist. He is a good man, a loyal preacher, and is doing good. May the Lord bless his work. More and better work for the Lord should be the desire and determination of all. Charles Holder.[83]

Boaz did return in July 1914 and held a successful meeting. He reported:

Bridgeport, Ala., May 30. The meeting began here last Lord's day. I began on Tuesday night. To date there have been thirteen baptisms and two from the denominations who had been scripturally baptized. Great crowds. Every business house is closing for the day services. Others expected yet to come. W. T. Boaz.[84]

This closes Bridgeport's church history. Bridgeport is still a viable congregation today—(2024).

DORAN'S COVE

Sometime soon after the Revolutionary War, John Woods, a Cherokee Indian, built a stone house just northeast of Russell's Cave. He was granted 640 acres which included Russell Cave as payment for his Revolutionary War service to the Americans. Major James Doran moved into the house and acquired the land. Maj. James Doran was supposedly married twice; first, to a daughter of Cherokee Indian Chief John Wood. Doran later sold the land to Thomas Russell. The land remained in the Russell family until 1928 when Oscar Ridley bought the land.

When the old stone house was built the walls were made of plaster. On one of the plastered walls in the house was found written "Andrew Jackson, May 15, 1813." As Jackson was the Indian commissioner, it is generally known that he drew up the agreement between Woods and Doran and that this writing was the date the agreement was drawn up.

Settlers began to come into the cove early. Eventually, enough spiritual-minded people were living there they began to desire to worship God according to the New Testament pattern. By the 1890s preachers began to come to Doran's Cove and preach the New Testament gospel to the people.

Richard Johnson is the first recorded preacher to preach the

New Testament pattern in Doran's Cove. The next was E. H. Boyd. Boyd came in late August of 1894 and conducted a gospel meeting. He reported the following picture of the work in the Cove:

> Jasper, Sept. 3. I have just closed a meeting in Doran's Cove, which resulted in eight addition to the one body. This is a comparatively new point. Brother Richard Johnson of Bridge-port, Ala., had been preaching here some, and had formed a nucleus to which the eight were added, making the work perma-nent at this point. He was with me in the meeting. E. H. Boyd. [85]

Boyd said this work was relatively new. Just how new we do not know but from what is stated it could have been from a few months old to a couple of years by the time Boyd made his first preaching tour to the Cove.

The next preacher to hold a meeting at Doran's Cove was Daniel Gunn. He came and held a meeting of nine days duration. The meeting began on August 17th and continued through August 25th. He reported eight baptisms and two restorations.[86]

J. H. Morton came and preached on the third (23) and fourth Lord's Day (30th) of 1896.[87] He also returned on the fifth Lord's Day of August. The *Gospel Advocate* gave no results on these three Sunday services. Then on the 26th he returned and began a gospel meeting.[88]

E. H. Boyd returned in 1899 and conducted a meeting for the congregation at Doran's Cove. He wrote from Doran's Cove, on September 26. During his meeting there: "I am at this place in a meeting, with good interest .... May God bless the work and all the workers."[89]

Six years later Flavil Hall of Trion, Georgia, came to Doran's Cove for a gospel meeting He wrote:

I began a meeting at Doran's Cove, Ala., on July 30 and continued it till August 7. There were three persons baptized. While there I made my home with Brother D. T. Crownover, a noble-hearted Christian, whose good wife and children are all with him in the gospel. The congregation treated me with all the kindness that a Christian should wish. They worship regularly on the Lord's day. My next meeting will be at Trenton, Ga. Flavil Hall.[90]

Four years after Hall's meeting, Charles Holder came to Doran's Cove and held a meeting. He described the meeting as follows:

I was in a meeting in Doran's Cove, near Orme, from the third Sunday to the fourth Sunday night in this month. Five were baptized. The interest and attendance were fine. Charles Holder. [91]

S. V. Geer reported that Holder baptized five at Doran's Cove during this meeting. Holder would return through the years and hold other meetings.[92]

Even though the next report is five years after our target date of 1914, it reveals a critical bit of information about Doran's Cove congregation. We therefore give Charles Martin's report in full:

Bridgeport, August 18.-From the fifth Sunday in July to Tuesday evening after the second Sunday in August, I was in good meetings at Doran's Cove, Ala., and Orme, Tenn., with large audiences and fine interest throughout the meetings. Eight made the confession and were baptized, and two Baptists and two Methodists learned "the way of the Lord more perfectly" and united with us on the Bible. The disciples at Doran's Cove agreed to keep house for the Lord and meet on the first day of the week for worship. The church at Orme is moving along nicely. Charles Martin.[93]

Martin's report revealed that the church had seemingly ceased to meet on the Lord's Day for worship. Notice the contrast between Orme and Doran's Cove. The Cove had ceased meeting and Orme "was moving along nicely."

This closes our designated period on Doran's Cove. We do report that in 2024 though small in number, it has weathered time to continue worshipping the Lord Jesus Christ to this day.

TRENTON

Trenton is a small unincorporated community in Jackson County, Alabama, United States. It is located nearly 8 miles east-northeast of Gurley in the Paint Rock Valley. In its early days, it was a thriving community. In September of 1901 E. L. Cambron came to Trenton and set up a tent. His meeting was a ten-day meeting. This was the first time Trenton was mentioned in the pages of the *Gospel Advocate*. It was to announce this tent meeting. It read as follows:

Garth. August 23—The tent meeting held at Trenton. Ala., by E. L. Cambron of Winchester, Tenn. began on the first Lord's day in August and continued for ten days. Trenton is a small place filled with ignorance and sectarianism. Before the meeting began the Baptists agreed at their Sunday school that they would not attend the meeting or allow any one that they could keep from attending. So, they all agreed not to attend, and some of them kept their vow and neither attended the meeting nor allowed their children to attend; others broke their vow and came out to the meeting. The result was that the Baptist minister and his wife heard the truth pure and simple and accepted the same. Two more Baptists followed, one Presbyterian, one (Christian) was reclaimed. and one came from the world. The Baptist minister was teaching school for the Baptists. They wanted to lock the door on him but were afraid. So, they stopped their children from school. I hope that much good will result from the meeting. Luther B. Jones.[94]

The Baptist preacher who was converted was John J. Horton. He would, through the next few years, hold several meetings for the church at Trenton. Probably the biggest event, however, to ever happen there was the debate between E. L. Cambron of the church of Christ and J. R. Lamb of the Missionary Baptists. It occurred in October 1902. The announcement through the pages of the *Gospel Advocate* stirred much excitement throughout Northeast Alabama. It read as follows:

> We are requested to announce that there will be a debate between E. L. Cambron (Christian) and J. K. (R.) Lamb (Missionary Baptist) at Trenton, Ala., beginning on October 20 and continuing six days. All are invited. Those who go by rail will get off at Paint Rock, Ala., or at Gurley, Ala. You will find brethren at these places.[95]

L. R. Sewell announced that he was helping Brother Cambron in the debate at Trenton, Alabama. He wrote:

> I am now assisting Brother Cambron in a debate at. Trenton, Ala. It is progressing nicely. The brethren are delighted."[96]

Sewell gave a detailed description of the debate, which we give in full:

> I went to Trenton, Ala., to assist Brother E. L. Cambron in a debate with J. R. Lamb, which began on October 20, at 9 A.M., and continued for six days.
>
> Six propositions were discussed. Brother Cambron affirmed

on the first proposition, which was: "The church of which I, E. L. Cambron, am a member, is apostolic in origin, doctrines and practice. He planted himself on the congregation at Winchester, Tenn., and, after finding the church in the New Testament, proceeded *to* show that that congregation taught and practiced just as they did in the New Testament.

On the second day Mr. Lamb, who is a good and pleasant speaker, affirmed on the same subject. His proposition was, "The Scriptures teach that the Missionary Baptist Church of Christ is apostolic in origin, doctrine, and practice."

Mr. Lamb is a shrewd man. He did not try to find the origin of the church, either as to time or place, but be said all he had to do was to find a church in the New Testament which baptized and did missionary work; then he would have a Missionary Baptist Church. It was replied that John was a Baptist because he, as a person, baptized; hence only those persons who baptize are Baptists. The church, as a whole, does not baptize; hence the church is not Baptist. Women do not baptize; hence it is wrong to call them "Baptista." Then Mormons baptize and do missionary work. Are Mormons Missionary Baptists? We baptize and do missionary work. Are we Missionary Baptists? After overturning all of Mr. Lamb's arguments, Brother Cambron proceeded to show many things taught and practiced by the Missionary Baptists that are not scriptural.

On the third day Mr. Lamb fought at a decided disadvantage. The proposition was "The Holy Scriptures are all-sufficient for the conversion of sinners, the perfection of saints, and the eternal salvation of Christians."

Brother Cambron did some masterly work on this proposition; and as Mr. Lamb would not commit himself to the abstract work of the Spirit, he could make no headway.

On the fourth day Mr. Lamb affirmed the impossibility• of apostasy. Brother Cambron again met and successfully overturned all Mr Lamb! s argument.

On the fifth day Brother Cambron affirmed baptism to a

penitent believer to be for, in order to, the remission of sins. On this proposition Brother Cambron did bis best work: while, as you will see, Mr. Lamb did absolutely nothing. Brother Cambron took the position that the Christian religion is a religion; that repentance and baptism are for the remission of sins because they are works of faith, bringing us into Christ, where we have redemption through his blood, the forgiveness of sins.

In his next Brother Cambron quoted Mark 16: 15, 16; Acts 2: 38; and Acts 22: 16, to show how baptism as an act of faith connects us with the promise of forgiveness of sins; then he confirmed it by the best scholars in the Baptist Church. Mr. Lamb then spoke twenty minutes, most of which time was spent in trying to extricate himself from an unfortunate admission he had made in a letter to Brother Cambron. Brother Cambron then spent his remaining thirty minutes in a general summing up of his arguments, to which Mr. Lamb made no reply at all, saying: 'I have nothing more to say.'

On the sixth day Mr. Lamb spent forty-five minutes in trying to prove that the Missionary Baptist Church has a scriptural right to withhold the Lord's Supper from all, except members of the same Missionary Baptist Church. But he went into this proposition with his hands tied, for, in a sermon preached by him on Lord's day before the debate began (which sermon we heard), he showed from the word of God that all children of God are kings and priests unto God, by virtue of which they have a scriptural right to all the blessings and privileges in the kingdom, or church, of the living God. Then he admitted, on his first proposition, that there are children of God that do not belong to the Missionary Baptist Church. Of course, this was all used against him with killing affect. Then it was shown that the Scriptures do not recognize any such thing as a Missionary Baptist Church, hence, do not grant to it any rights at all. Here the debate closed. But before Brother Cambron took his seat, a very intelligent man arose and demanded of him to be baptized, using the language of the Ethiopian to Philip. Brother

Cambron then announced that we would go at once to the water, but another man said, "Wait till I go and get my clothes; I wish to be baptized, too." We then announced that the baptizing would take place at 2 P.M. Almost the entire audience went with us to the water, where I baptized the two men and the wife of one of them. Thus, closed one of the most pleasant and successful debates I ever attended. Bridgeport, Ala. L. R. Sewell. [97]

As to when the congregation was established or who established it is unknown only to our Lord. It could have been established with the tent meeting by Cambron or it could have been an infant church at the time of the tent meeting was conducted.

This debate gave the church at Trenton a big boost of spiritual energy. Sewell reported three baptisms as a direct result of the debate. No wonder Sewell it was "one of the most pleasant and successful debates" he had ever attended. Cambron returned to Trenton in the fall of 1905 to hold a meeting. The Saturday on which Cambron began the meeting at Trenton was October 8, 1905.[98] We never found the results of that meeting.

J. J. Horton of Elora, Tennessee had only been a Christian nine years when he came and held an eleven days' meeting at Trenton in 1910. The meeting was a success. More than just a report on a meeting, Horton gave some historical information also. He wrote a very good report on the situation at Trenton:

Elora, August 7... On July 23 I closed an eleven-days' meeting at Trenton, Jackson County, Ala., at the water's edge, with twelve baptized and one from the Baptists. Trenton is a strong sectarian place-mostly Baptists and Presbyterians; and the church or Christ was so weak and became discouraged last year and stopped keeping house for the Lord. Having heard of their condition, and it being in the sacred spot close to where [was raised (and I was raised to believe the Baptist Church was the church, and my dear father had preached for them fifteen years),

I determined by the help of the Lord to go into the camp of the enemy of the simple truths of the gospel, who disbelieve the power of the gospel to save. So, I went into the work with Brother Ace Hill to lead the singing for me, which he did nobly. 1 was led to expect a freeze out; but I am thankful. With all the rain we had during the meeting, we had a packed house every night; so, I had the opportunity to teach them the simple gospel, which man, of them had never heard before. So, the meeting closed with our little band strengthened and ready to again keep house for the Lord in his appointed way. I shall continue to preach for them during the coming winter as often as I can, to teach them "the way of the Lord more perfectly." J. J. Horton. [99]

Horton's mother still lived in this community and, at the time, was still a member of the Missionary Baptist church.

A brother W. E. Jackson inquired of E. G. Sewell at the *Gospel Advocate* concerning the use of wine in the communion. A Missionary Baptist minister at Trenton raised this question so, Jackson tried to get an answer. The inquiry read:

Brother Sewell: We have an elder of the Missionary Baptist Church at this place who says he will no longer take wine at the Lord's table, and that it is a sin to even look upon it if it is fermented, using Num. 6 for an argument. He said to me that he did not see how I could afford to offer it to the people, or the church of Christ. "'How can you afford to offer it to me?'" he asked. I said: "You must not open your mouth and swallow all that men give you." I try to lead the small congregation at this place on Lord's day, but do not offer any one the cup further than Christ did when he instituted the Supper and gave it to his disciples. The Baptist brother said he had asked some Baptist publishing company to give him one Bible authority to use fermented wine at the Lord's table, and they say they have none. Trenton, Ala. W. E. Jackson.[100]

This was a controversy that was being raised throughout the various religious groups. It was interesting that a Missionary Baptist asked one of our brethren for an answer.

Brother J. J. Horton returned to Trenton and conducted a meeting in October 1911. The result was given in the *Gospel Advocate*:

> Brother J. J. Horton's meeting at Trenton, Ala., continued eight days and closed with five baptized and one from the Methodists who had previously been immersed.[101]

Horton also returned for another meeting in 1912. This meeting proved to be an interesting one as we shall see. Horton had grown up in this area and still had family living near Trenton. W. E. Jackson wrote the following:

> Brother W. E. Jackson writes from Trenton, Ala.: "Brother J. J. Horton, of Atlanta, Ga., began a meeting at this place on the second Lord's day in July and continued it twelve days, with good interest. Brother J. M. Gainer, of Scottsboro, Ala., was also with us the latter part of the meeting and continued the meeting three days after Brother Horton left. This was one of the grandest meetings ever held in this valley. The meeting closed with two baptisms and three from the Missionary Baptists. Of these latter, one is Brother Horton's mother, who is about eighty years of age; another, the mother-in-law of the writer, who is seventy-six years of age; and the other, one of my sisters-in-law, a married lady. 'We are so glad to have all of these added to the little congregation here.'[102]

It is interesting that Horton's mother, Anne, was finally baptized at the end of this meeting. Horton had been a gospel preacher for some years and his mother finally decides to obey the gospel. When Horton began the Trenton meeting in July, he was engaged in a work with S. H. Hall in Atlanta, Georgia. His wife became very ill, so he severed that work and moved back to Elora, Tennessee in December 1912.

He immediately began preaching on what seemed to be a circuit and Trenton was part of it. He gave a glimpse of the situation with his wife and his life by April 15, 1913:

> Elora, Tenn., April 15.—I wish to say to the loyal brotherhood that since, on account of my wife's ill health, I was forced to sever my connection with Brother S. H. Hall in the Atlanta work (which I regretted very much to have to do) the last of December 1912, and return to my former home in Elora, Tenn., I am not in the retired list by any means, but I am preaching two and three times every Lord's day, notwithstanding my wife's health is no better. My time is all engaged until late in the fall; so, you see I am not advertising for meetings. Last Lord's day I preached at Trenton, Ala., at 11 A.M.; at Garth, at 3 P.M.; at Paint Rock, at 7: 30 P.M. One young lady made the good confession at the night service, and I baptized her into Christ on Monday morning. May the good work continue in the name of our Savior. J. J. Horton.[103]

In September he held another meeting at Trenton. There were no additions; but he said, "The interest was good." J. J. Horton. [104] This was the last report concerning Trenton, by Horton in the *Gospel Advocate*. In fact, it was the last report of any kind about the work at Trenton, until March 1917. J. M. McCaleb reported on his contributions to his work in Japan. Trenton donated $15 in December 1916.[105]

McCaleb's report was the final report in the *Gospel Advocate* concerning the work at Trenton. We do not know what became of the work. Did it change its name? Did it merge with another congregation, or did it just fade into the past, never to be seen or heard of again?

The church had been very active while Cambron was coming on a regular basis. When he stopped coming the congregation back set back tremendously. Then for eight or nine years the work did very little, but in 1910 when John J. Horton came on the scene the church began to take on new life. Horton's medical practice began to take a great deal of his time. He was not the kind who was doctoring for the money. He never turned anyone away. His heart was with the poor of his area. S. H. Hall wrote of him:

> ... Dr. Horton labored with us in Atlanta, Ga., for one year as medical evangelist, preaching on Lord's days, holding meetings in and near the city, and doing gratis all of our medical service for the poor. This was one of the happiest years of my life, and one in which I felt we came more nearly meeting the demands of New Testament teaching in local church work. On account of his wife's health, he had to give up this work and returned to Elora, where he lived most of the time until the end come ....[106]

Horton began to have health issues that would eventually cause his work to end. When he was in his last days T. C. Little managed to get the church in Fayetteville, Tennessee, where Little preached, to give Horton $50 dollars to help pay his expenses. Thus, we see that Horton was not trying to get wealthy from his medical practice. He was a humanitarian and most of all—a true Christian. Along with his death, it seems perhaps Trenton died also.

WOODVILLE

Woodville is a town in Jackson County, Alabama, United States. It was officially established by an act of the Alabama State Legislature on December 13, 1819, one day before Alabama became a state. It was later incorporated on May 12, 1890; but lost its charter in 1897. It was reincorporated in 1912.

There is no evidence that there was a New Testament church in Woodville in 1885, but there was a gospel preacher living in or near Woodville at that time. He was F. M. Wallace, and he was preaching in that area.[107] The first real proof of the Woodville congregation came from W. H. Dixon. He wrote:

> I have just returned from Kennermer (Kennamers) Cove, Marshall Co., Ala, where I preached eight sermons, Bro. Joe. Jones, one. Good interest but only one baptism. I also preached one sermon, "preach the word!" at Woodville, Jackson County, Ala., to a large congregation. The people in that part of the state are anxious to hear. I could not stay long; I hope to be able to return again soon ... W. H. Dixon.[108]

This reveals that the church was at least in a formative stage by the time Dixon came and preached in the summer of 1889.

The next note to mention Woodville was written by J. R. Kennamer, of Woodville. He just mentioned in the *Gospel Advocate* how much he appreciated the gospel paper.[109] He is reported as living in or near Woodville, Alabama.

R. N. Moody was the next make a report on Woodville. He gave a very brief report. It read—"Woodville, Ala., 15 discourses; fine attendance and good interest."[110]

After having closed an eight-day meeting at Trenton, John J. Horton held a meeting at Garth. Upon closing that meeting, he came and preached on sermon at Woodville. We give his report on the work at Woodville:

> Elora, Tenn., August 27; I preached to the faithful little band of workers at Woodville, Ala., on Lord's-day evening. who have set other churches a good example about how to build a church house. Three good brethren saw bow much help they could get from the little band, and they saw they must have six hundred dollars more; so, they just paid it themselves, making quite a sacrifice to do it, to keep from having to appeal to the brotherhood for help... J. J. Horton.
> [111]

He returned and preached at Woodville in March 1914, although he never made a report. It was reported by C. Petty of Huntsville Petty wrote of Dr. Horton:

> Dr. Horton passed through town last Saturday on his way to Woodville, Ala., to preach. He is busy preaching "the unsearchable riches." C. Petty.[112]

Brother J. R. Kennamer sent eight names as subscribers to the *Gospel Advocate* in June of 1914. He was still listed as living at Woodville.[113] Within a few weeks of Kennamer's report L. B. Jones gave a brief statement as to the work at Woodville. He wrote "I am now in a good meeting at this place." L. B. Jones.[114] A week later he give another report on the results of the meeting. The report read:

> Winchester, July 11.—My meeting at Woodville, Ala., closed on Friday night, with seven baptized. L. B. Jones.[115]

Jones returned for another meeting in 1915 and another one in1916. He, by then, had risen to the top of the list at Woodville as their choice for a meeting preacher. This closes our early history of the Woodville church. It is still active in the Lord's kingdom in the year of our Lord 2024.

GARTH

Garth is a community that is located about four- and one-half miles northeast of Gurley, Alabama. The first indication that the gospel was preached at Garth came in a report from Charles L. Talley:

> ... the writer preached two years ago, baptized twelve, and aroused the brethren to activity, which resulted in the construction of a much-needed house and Lord's day housekeeping. They are yet following in Bible path and duty.[116]

Talley's report was published in 1897 and he said that he had preached at Garth two years before. That would place the earliest account of preaching at Garth in 1895.

The first contemporary report came from J. L. Hucks in 1896. The report was short but informative. Hucks wrote:

> Garth, Sept. 19.—I am in a good meeting at this place. One has been baptized, and there is another to be baptized Sunday morning. We trust there will be others before we close. J. L. Hucks. [117]

In the next report on the same meeting, Hucks informs us that the congregation is called "Cedar Point." The report reads:

> Maysville, Oct. 3. I began a series of meetings with the brethren at Cedar Point, Jackson County, Ala., Saturday night before the second Lord's day in September, and continued until the third Lord's day. The immediate result was that two Methodists concluded to put on Christ by being buried with him in baptism. Considering the busy time of picking cotton and saving fodder, it was one of the best meetings of my life. The singing was first-class. The Lord willing, I will preach for them again next year. J. L. Hucks.[118]

Hucks did return the next year for another meeting. The work at Garth kept drawing Hucks back. Maybe he was the person who began this work. In his report, which was typically Hucks, very brief:

> Maysville, Aug. 2: On Saturday night before the third Lord's day in July I began a meeting with the brethren at Garth, in Jackson County, and continued until Friday night following, with one addition to the one body.[119]

Charles L. Talley came during this meeting and preached one sermon. He described it as follows:

> Recently I made two trips to Alabama and visited Paint Rock, Kennamer Cove, and Garth, and kindly asked to hold a missionary meeting at Lim Rock. I preached one sermon at Garth (Cedar Point), and left Brother Hucks in a very interesting meeting that lasted about eight days, one taking membership. About one month later, Brother Boyd, of Jasper, Tenn., held another week's meeting, with one addition. The above place is where the writer preached two years ago, baptized

twelve, and aroused the brethren to activity, which resulted in the construction of a much-needed house and Lord's day house-keeping. They are yet following in Bible path and duty. Charles L. Talley.[120]

Talley mentions a house of worship having been built at Garth. Apparently, the congregation was becoming very active as a New Testament church. Later that same month J. R. Bradley travelled from Booneville, Tennessee to Paint Rock Valley on an exploratory preaching tour. He preached one sermon at Garth. [121] By December, he was planning to move to Gurley and take a preaching circuit for four churches. His report gave the details:

> Booneville, Dec. 8.—After this week please send my paper to Gurley, Ala. Please announce in the Advocate that our address is changed from Booneville, Tenn., to that place. Wife and I both dislike to leave Tennessee. We are Tennesseans by birth. Please say to our brethren, sisters, and friends of our native old State: "God be with you till we meet again." Four congregations in Alabama: Kennamer Cove, Whitaker's Chapel, Paint Rock, and Garth —have invited us to their field of labor. There is no society or clique of men moving us in this work, but just simply an agreement, these earnest workers and myself agreeing together to cultivate that field.[122]

Now Garth would have regular preaching at least once a month. In those days, a congregation might go for a month or two and have no preaching. Bradley continued to work in the valley until 1900. While Bradley was in this section of northeast Alabama, John E. Dunn came into the valley and held meetings for various congregations. Some of them were the churches for which J.R. Bradley was preaching. Dunn wrote of Bradley's work in the valley:

Garth, September 11. —I am at this writing in Paint Rock Valley
(Ala.), preaching. I will be in this section till October 15. I am
having good audiences and splendid attention. There were eight
confessions the first week. I am expecting good results from
these meetings, judging from present indications. This has been
a neglected field, but now Brother J. R. Bradley is doing a good
work here. John E. Dunn.[123]

You notice that Dunn was at Garth when he wrote this
report. No doubt Garth was one of the congregations for which
Dunn preached a gospel meeting.

Within a few months, Bradley moved back to Lincoln
County, Tennessee. He was definitely back by May 4, 1900,
because he signed a deed on that date.[124]

The next report on the work, after Bradley returned to
Tennessee, was made by Luther B. Jones, a native son of Garth.
During Bradley's ministry in Paint Rock Valley, Jones was away
training at Nashville Bible School to preach. He attended the
Nashville Bible School reunion in 1906, which is proof of his
attendance at the school.[125]

John E. Dunn had this to say about the promising young
Luther B. Jones:

In this connection I wish to say (a number of Alabama friends
with whom I have talked about this work will read these lines) to
Northeast Alabama friends, you have in your midst Brother
Luther B. Jones, of Garth, Ala. He is a good young man of fine
ability. You could hardly find a more acceptable preacher. He
loves his own people, they are his kindred in the flesh, and he
prefers to spend his life at work, among his own people. Take
hold of him, keep him at work, encourage and support him. By a
long and active life in your own country good results will follow.
Taking up one home man and using him will open up the way
for others. Several of you have asked me to find you a good man
to work in that country. I most heartily commend unto you

Luther B. Jones. You can address him at Garth, Ala. John E. Dunn.[126]

After J. R. Bradley left the valley, Jones became the preacher for Garth. He gave this report on a meeting held by E. H. Boyd:

Garth, September 11. Brother E. H. Boyd, of Jasper, Tenn., closed a meeting at this place last night which resulted in seventeen additions. All made the good confession and were baptized, and the meeting closed with good interest. Success to all who are preaching the gospel of Christ. Luther B. Jones.[127]

E. H. Boyd made a separate report on the meeting, which included additional information:

Jasper, September 14. I am just home from a meeting at Garth, Ala., where I preached sixteen sermons and baptized seventeen persons upon a confession of their faith in Christ. Our young brother, Luther Jones, was With me all the time (this being his home), and he, in connection with others, led the song service. The meeting was regarded as one of the best in the history of this congregation, and the good that it will accomplish eternity alone can reveal. E. H. Boyd.[128]

Boyd revealed more information about L. B. Jones. He confirms that he was a native of Garth and he was capable of leading singing also. Boyd said he aided in the song services during this meeting.

On August 23, 1901, Jones reported on a meeting held by E.L. Cambron at Garth. Cambron had just closed a meeting at nearby Trenton. Jones reported on both the meetings. We give the portion that relates to Garth:

After the meeting closed at Trenton, Brother Cambron came to Garth and held a few days' meeting. The result was one addition.

The weather was so bad that the people could not get out to church. I believe Brother Cambron has done much good in this neighborhood. Churches in this county, as far as I know, are poor and untaught, especially on giving. It would be well for those that support the gospel in destitute fields to remember a brother when he labors in such a field as this. May the Lord help us all to speak where the Bible speaks and to remain silent where it is silent. Luther B. Jones.[129]

After Cambron's meeting nothing was reported in the *Gospel Advocate* for another nine years. What was the problem? They had their own home-grown college educated preacher. Did he just not report on the work at Garth? Was he holding so many meetings that he was not home very much? We know he was preaching in meetings as far south as Highland Home, Crenshaw County, Alabama.[130] We know he was still living at Garth in 1907.[131] Could it be that his absence allowed Garth to grow laxed in their duties toward the Lord? Something brought on nine years of silence.

Jones returned to hold a meeting in 1910. This was the first report to break the long silence. The report simply read: "Brother Jones is now in a meeting at Garth, Ala."[132]

J. M. Gainer came to Garth for a meeting in 1912. He reported that he had: "1 addition; Garth, Ala., 3 baptisms, 3 restorations, and 1 from denominations."[133]

The final report within our parameter of time (1914) was sent to the *Gospel Advocate* by J. J. Horton. His report was short it read:

Elora, Tenn., August 27. I closed an eight-days' meeting at Trenton, Ala., on the third Lord's day in August. The interest was good, but there were no additions. I also closed an eight-days' meeting at Garth, Ala., on the fourth Lord's-day morning, with fine interest and four added by obedience to the gospel ... J. J. Horton.[134]

Horton had grown to manhood in Trenton which was only three and a half miles from Garth. He was considered a native son to the folks at Garth. Horton's report closed our study on Garth. One side note—in the first two or three reports Garth was also called Cedar Point. That, however, ceased when a community and a congregation in Madison County were established.

STEVENSON

In 1859, a county election was held to determine whether a new courthouse should be more centrally located in Stevenson or Scottsboro. Stevenson was chosen but the Civil War nullified this action, and the matter was not settled until 1868. On September 5, 1868, the Commissioners Court met in Bellefonte and voted to remove the county seat from Bellefonte to Scottsboro, named for its founder Robert T. Scott, a native of North Carolina. Stevenson had missed its chance to become the most important community in Jackson County, Alabama. It would become important in another way. The Lord's church would be established there in the late 1800's.

The earliest reference to Christians living in the Stevenson area was recorded in the *Gospel Advocate* on July 20, 1893. It was written by J. D. Gunn. The short report stated:

> Scottsboro, July 10, 1898. I am now on the way to Stevenson, Ala. to be with Brother J D. Jones in a meeting at that place. J. D. Gunn.[135]

J. D. Gunn gave a fuller report on the Stevenson meeting. He also gave an interesting report on Cedar Grove, a community about two miles west of Stevenson. Apparently, from the information we have, the Cedar Grove community did not have an established New Testament church at that time. He preached in Cedar Grove after the meeting at Stevenson closed. We give the report in full:

> Bell Factory, August 13. Brother J. D. Jones and I closed a meeting at Stevenson, Ala., on Saturday night, July 15th. No additions, but a good interest. On Lord's day I preached at Cedar Grove, about two miles from Stevenson, which resulted in one reclaimed and one from the Adventists. I preached in the Advent church house. The brethren at that place promised to meet on the Lord's day and worship God in his appointed ways ... J.D. Gunn.[136]

D. L. G. Wilson, who would later become an elder, sent a question to the *Gospel Advocate*. He was concerned about the practice of "sprinkling or pouring" being taught in the Stevenson area. The Christians in the area needed answers to problems such as this. Wilson's question was as follows:

> Brother Lipscomb: Will you please answer a question for me through the Advocate or by letter? Then, is a preacher in this section who is preaching sprinkling and pouring. He says it is the only proper mode of baptism; he also says that he is a Christian preacher and an elder in the church of Christ. What should the church of Christ do with him? Should the elders permit him to preach such doctrine in their churches? I am a Christian anti a member of the church of Christ, but not a subscriber of the Advocate; so please send me a copy containing question and answer. D. L. G. Wilson, Stevenson, Ala.[137]

Lipscomb knew the man who was teaching these things in the Stevenson area. He wrote the reply:

The man who is doing this is Haden, of course. He once wrote me that all the dictionaries and lexicons define "baptize" to sprinkle or pour. Whenever I met Haden, he was hunting money. I wrote him that if he would show the Methodists and Presbyterians one of these lexicons, they would give him all the money he needed. They had long desired and sought such a lexicon and had not been able to find it. Haden impressed me outside of this that he was along this line if you think it is worth answering. like "Bob" Taylor's teacher that was prepared to teach the world was flat or round, as the people desired. I suppose those who like such teaching would be pleased with him; but. Christians ought not for a moment to think of fellow-shipping a man as a teacher so ignorant as this. If he is a fair man and believes this, he would go to churches that believe this.[138]

This demonstrates the desire to grow in the truth. At later times someone from Stevenson asks questions of the *Gospel Advocate* staff and answers will be given. The few scattered Christians thirsted and hungered after spiritual truths. They were on their way to becoming an established work. They so desired to have an established congregation that they resorted to pleading with other brethren to help them in a thirty day's meeting as the report below will show:

What congregation, or number of congregations, will unite with us to have a meeting of thirty days held at Stevenson, Ala.? Stevenson is a small town of four or five hundred inhabitants, situated at the junction of the Nashville, Chattanooga and St. Louis Railway and the Southern Railway, where there has never been a meeting held by the church of God. This place is, I think, a fine missionary point. There is no congregation here, but a few brethren, well scattered, that think nothing can be done without a preacher. I want a meeting here sometime during the fall. Who will help? W. J. Rorex, Stevenson, Ala.[139]

W. J. Rorex will eventually become one of the first elders to be appointed at Stevenson. He tells us that in July 1900 there was no congregation at Stevenson. He had already begun to write short articles in the *Gospel Advocate*. He demonstrated that he had leadership ability and was trusted by the community. Lipscomb described Rorex as a "drummer."[140] That was an old southern term that meant a traveling salesman. That is how Rorex supported his family. Rorex wrote a short article about a denominational preacher who held a lengthy meeting and did not tell the people how to get salvation from their sins. His complaint was:

> Mr. Joe Colwell, Cumberland Presbyterian preacher, of Huntsville, Ala., recently conducted a meeting at this place, lasting some ten or twelve days. In this meeting he did not invite penitent believers to the anxious sent, or mourner's bench to pray and be prayed for I would ask: Why was this? Have the Cumberland Presbyterians abandoned the prayer system of getting religion, and are they coming more to the scriptural teaching? As I understand that they had no conversions, is that the reason? It was not because they did not have a good preacher; for their members say Mr. Colwell is the best, or one of the best, in the State. There was one thing, however, that he was careful not to do, and that was to tell the unconverted what to do to be saved. It seems to me that a meeting of ten days-and that, too, for the purpose of saving souls--should have at least one sermon on so important a theme as "What must I do to be saved?" All scriptural doctrine was conspicuously avoided, however, during the meeting. Stevenson, Ala. W. J. Rorex.[141]

S. R. Logue came to Stevenson in 1902 and held a gospel meeting. In his report he gives a clue as to when the Stevenson church was established. His article gave a vivid picture of this infant congregation as can be seen below:

Lynnville, July 21. I have just closed an interesting and, I trust, profitable-tent meeting at Stevenson, Ala. The meeting continued nearly two weeks, with increasing interest. Brother John T. Glenn, of the Nashville Bible School, ably assisted by leading the song service. A congregation of worshipers was started here more than a year ago. and they have been faithful in the work of the Lord. The zeal and liberality of this little band are truly commendable. It is "pleasure to be among them." Two souls were baptized into Christ, and the seed of the kingdom was bountifully sown; saints were exhorted and encouraged, and sinners were warned "to flee from the wrath to come." S. R. Logue.[142]

Logue stated in his report that "A congregation of worshipers was started here more than a year ago." That would have happened between July 1900, when Rorex said, "There is no congregation here, but a few brethren, well scattered ..." and July 1902 when Logue stated that the church "started here more than a year ago."[143] Therefore, we place the establishment of the Stevenson work sometime early in 1901, in order to fit the information given by Logue.

Within two more years, the church is trying to get a building constructed. A message from the elders at Stevenson was published in the *Gospel Advocate* in July 1904 requesting help on building at Stevenson. The appeal was published with the following message:

Brethren W. J. Rorex, D. G. L. Wilson, and W. W. Wilson, elders of the church of Christ at Stevenson, Ala., send us the following statement, with a request that we publish it: "The church of Christ at Stevenson, Ala., has bought a lot on which to build a house of worship. We also have about twenty-five dollars in the treasury for building purposes, a part of which was donated by the following: Sister Margaret McFarland, $5; church at Viola, Tenn., $10.90. Should other churches and brethren O desire to have fellowship with us in this work, they can send their contributions to Miss Ophelia Wilson, treasurer of the church."[144]

There are some interesting items contained in the appeal. For instance, their treasurer was the sister of D. G. L. and W. W. Wilson who were elders at Stevenson. Secondly, they had purchased a lot on which to build; but only had $25 in their treasury. They must have had a deep faith to venture out on a building project with so little money saved. They must have believed strongly in God and the brethren.

During the same time as the appeal was being made a tent meeting was in progress at Stevenson. It was conducted by S. R. Logue and J. D. Gunn, who led the singing. It was reported that they had "good interest and are hopeful of good results from their labors."[145] Unfortunately, no report was ever found on the results of the meeting.

Little bits of information trickled down to help us reconstruct a partial history of the work at Stevenson. The next information was published in the form of a statement about a visit by W. J. Rorex to the offices of the *Gospel Advocate*. In the statement, Rorex is said to have given a "favorable report on the church at Stevenson.[146]

In early fall brother E. H. Boyd, of Dayton, Tenn., began a meeting at Stevenson, Ala., on Saturday evening, September 8. [147] The results of this meeting were not published until February 1907 and the report was made by J. L. Daniel. It simply stated that Boyd had held a meeting at Stevenson with one addition.[148]

Boyd returned in December for at least one sermon, because he converted a young man of twenty-five years who lived in Stevenson. In the young man's obituary is found the following statement:

> On Sunday morning, February 24, 1907, the death angel claimed one of the little band of disciples who worshiped with the church at Stevenson, Ala. Lem Gillem Wilson, youngest son

of D. L. G. and Paralee Wilson. He was twenty-five years old. He
was baptized into Christ by Brother E. H. Boyd on December
24, 1906, just eight weeks before his death, and he never failed to
meet with the church on Lord's day during his short but useful
life as a Christian ... W. J. Rorex.[149]

Boyd became one of the favorite preachers in northeast
Alabama. His lessons moved young Lem Wilson to become a
Christian. You may have noticed that his father was one of the
three elders at Stevenson.

By March 1909, the congregation was engaged in building a
house of worship. In an article written by W. J. Rorex, it was
stated in the following way:

> The brethren here are now building a house of worship, which
> we are pushing a long to completion as fast as the weather will
> permit. We have contracted for a house to cost fourteen hundred
> dollars and hope to build as neat a house as possible for that
> money. We have cash on hand to the amount of eight hundred
> dollars, all told to date ....[150]

It was further stated:

> Should other churches or individuals wish to fellowship us in
> the work here, we would appreciate it very much indeed. I will
> say, for the benefit of those who wish to know, that we have
> the restrictive clause in our deed to the property. We are
> thankful indeed and are under many obligations to those who
> have been so kind and liberal to help us so far in this work.
> [151]

The restrictive clause Rorex mentioned was placed in the deed
that forbids the use of instrumental music in worship and the use
of societies to do the church's work.

In May F. W. Smith conducted a meeting at Stevenson with

"excellent attendance." The meeting closed with four baptisms.
[152]

The building was nearing completion by the first of May 1909. The next report gave the details:

> The new house of worship at Stevenson, Ala., has been completed, all except the seats .... The church here is indeed thankful for the liberal thank offerings which we have secured from the brethren and churches.
>
> We have eleven hundred dollars and have borrowed three hundred dollars to finish paying the contractors who, we are glad to say, have built us a nice, neat, comfortable house, and who gave us good, honest work. The above expenses are for the house unseated. We will have an additional expense for seats and light.
> [153]

The church began to prosper a little economically, and some members wanted to help other congregations and other good causes. Miss Orphia Wilson. Stevenson, Ala., sent a dollar to the school in Georgia that S. H. Hall was supporting—the McCravy Orphan's Home and Bible School.[154] This spirit continued for some time as will be seen in later years.

Our next reference to Stevenson came in the form of a question to Lipscomb again. A brother, W. B. Brown, had asked questions before. This time it seemed that there was a disagreement over whether a congregation had the right to appoint elders and deacons. The question was written as:

> Brother Lipscomb: Is it right for a congregation to ordain deacons and elders? Paul said he left Titus in Crete to "ordain elders in every city." (Tit.1: 5.) Whose duty is it now to ordain? In fact, is it any one's duty to do so? Stevenson, Ala. W. B. Brown.[155]

Lipscomb answered in typical Lipscomb fashion. He could

not tolerate people asking questions that had already been discussed through the pages of the *Gospel Advocate*. This was one of those questions. So, Lipscomb just referred Brown to former answers by giving Brown months and days, where the answers could be found.[156]

Our next report comes from J. M. McCaleb, who was a missionary to Japan. While raising funds in Chattanooga among the churches in that city, he was invited to come to Stevenson. He gave the following on the church at Stevenson:

> Stevenson is between Chattanooga and Nashville. Here we have about twenty brethren who have lately erected a very neat, commodious house, costing fifteen hundred dollars, with a capacity to seat two hundred and fifty people. Dr. Rorex says people who try can do anything.[157]

From this information we learn an approximate time for the completion for the church building and the exact cost of construction. He also gave the capacity of the building and the approximate number of members at Stevenson. It was interesting that a missionary has given more specific details about a congregation he is only visiting for a short time than most reports give that are made by the local members.

G. Dallas Smith and William G. Klingman held a two-week meeting at Stevenson in 1913. Klingman gave a very vivid picture of the congregation during their time at Stevenson that year. On July 13 he wrote:

> Brother G. Dallas Smith and I began a meeting here two weeks ago and had a very good meeting. The brethren here have a very good house; and though the congregation is small in number, it is one of the most active and zealous churches we have anywhere. There was one addition by baptism, which brought much rejoicing. The field is not in a ripe condition for a large ingathering, but we believe that the "pure seed of the kingdom"

was forcibly and earnestly presented and received in a very kind spirit. Many of the sectarian neighbors came regularly, and one of their preachers came frequently, and seemed to enjoy the meetings. Brethren, let us remember that ripping, rearing, charging, pitching, and fighting the gospel into the sectarians, taking "all the hide off" as we go, is not the "winning spirit." But, as in every other walk of life, the spirit of the Master prevails and succeeds always. William G. Klingman.[158]

In December of that year W. J. Rorex of Stevenson, made an appeal through the pages of the *Gospel Advocate* on behalf of the brethren in Washington D.C. It stated:

Brother W. J Rorex, of Stevenson, Ala., writes as follows in reference to the appeal made in the Gospel Advocate of November 20 by Brother J. M. W. Gibson, of Washington, D. C.:

The little congregation in the picturesque town of Stevenson, Ala., nestling at the foothills of the great Cumberland Mountain, with its many beautiful and grand canyons and its diversified plateaus, notwithstanding her poverty, is ever on the lookout for more and greater opportunities for doing good and helping to spread the gospel and establish primitive Christianity in destitute fields and seeing the appeal in the Gospel Advocate from Brother Gibson at our nation's capital, this congregation now desires to have fellowship with the brethren there also. So, we want to say to Brother Gibson and the congregation at Washington, through the columns of the Gospel Advocate, that they can draw on the treasury of the little congregation at Stevenson for ten dollars, when needed, for the purchase of the property mentioned in the Advocate of November 20. We take this method for the reason that it may stimulate other churches to accept this work. This appeals to some of us as being a work that should be accomplished, and we would like to see this work pushed by every congregation where the Advocate is read. So, come along. brethren. And let

us secure this property for the brethren in our nation's capital.
[159]

This demonstrated the desire of the church at Stevenson to help other struggling congregations. Stevenson knew the struggles they had in getting started as a small group desiring to worship God in their own house of worship.

In July of the following year, Rorex made another appeal. This time it was for a tent to be used in a meeting in Pine Bluff, Arkansas. We give the appeal in full:

> At Pine Bluff, Ark., there are three loyal members-two sisters and one brother. They have been and are yet trying to have a preacher come there and hold a meeting but have failed to get a house of any kind in I which to hold the meeting. They were refused the courthouse. So, in order to have a meeting, they will have to secure a tent. They have the promise of a preacher as soon as they can get the tent. The church at Stevenson, Ala., has agreed to assist some in this meeting, and I am writing this to try and find a congregation that will furnish a tent. Pine Bluff is a city of some fifteen or twenty thousand souls, and the three brethren there need help in this work. Who will come to their rescue? What other congregation will help in establishing the cause there? Stevenson, Ala.[160]

The spirit of helping other brethren was one of the identifying marks of the Stevenson congregation.

G. Dallas Smith returned for another meeting in October 1914. The report was very short reference and was one of two communications reported in the *Gospel Advocate* for the year 1914.[161] With this brief communication from Smith, we close the early history of the church of Christ at Stevenson, Alabama.

SCOTTSBORO

Scottsboro is the largest town in Jackson County, Alabama. It became the official county seat. On September 5, 1868, the Commissioners Court met in Bellefonte and voted to remove the county seat from Bellefonte to Scottsboro, named for its founder Robert T. Scott, a native of North Carolina. In November 1868, county records were moved from Bellefonte to a small brick house in Scottsboro rented by Probate Judge David Tate.

Fourteen years later a brother writing from Scottsboro said:

> There are 800 or 1,000 people in that town, and that but few out of the number have had opportunity of hearing the ancient gospel, and he is very anxious for some preacher who can preach the plain truth —the word of the Lord —to pay them a visit and proclaim the gospel to that people. Who will go? [162]

The brother who made the request for some preacher to come and preach to them was no doubt W. J. Rorex, as he was said to be the only male member in Scottsboro. [163] Later that month D. M. Breaker of Chattanooga, Tennessee, came and held a gospel meeting for the scattered members in Scottsboro. Nov. 27th, 1882. He gave a very good report on his meeting:

I have just returned from Scottsboro, Ala., where I delivered a series of sermons, setting forth the ancient gospel as distinguished from the teachings of the different sects. The results are by no means satisfactory to me; yet I believe that some good has been affected. I found it impossible to secure a congregation—such a congregation as I think I should have had. Those who did attend, listened with fixed attention, and two or three expressed themselves as being thoroughly convinced; but no one obeyed the gospel. "Bad weather" may be assigned as one reason for not getting a large congregation, but I am satisfied it resulted mainly from prejudice, excited by the usual misrepresentation of our teachings. I was told by several persons that my congregations were larger than they expected. We have no organization in Scottsboro, and there are only four members in the place—three of whom are females. There are a few brethren in the surrounding country. I wish to mention particularly Elders Joseph Wheeler and James Daniel, both of whom are highly respected in the community. Bro. W. J. Rorex, the only male member in town, is a noble man, and an earnest Christian. He is a dentist and is also engaged in mercantile business. He and his excellent wife made me comfortable and happy during my abode with them. I had the pleasure of seeing a good deal of Eld. D. C. Coulson, pastor of the Baptist church and was much pleased with him. Our meeting was held in the Baptist church house.— D. M. Breaker, Chattanooga, Tenn. Nov. 27th, 1882.[164]

Breaker informed us that "there are only four members in the place—three of whom are females" and only one male member— W.J. Rorex. For a while, the desire for a congregation in Scottsboro would not materialize. The small group would not give up their hope.

In January V. M. Metcalfe travelled through Scottsboro and delivered two sermons. His experience there is worth giving below:

At Scottsboro, I spoke twice in the Baptist house to a fair audience. We have only a few disciples at this place. They have bought a lot and framing lumber enough to build them a house of worship. A little help will be very acceptable just at this stage. Brethren Rorex & Co. will be pleased to take charge of such funds and entertain all poor preachers who come that way. Bro. R. is a good man; call and see him. At this place I met Dr. Breaker, of Chattanooga. I was much pleased with him as an earnest man who was coming to the light and wanted to do good. He is a man of more than ordinary ability, and wants to preach the gospel, is anxious to work in this field, but we have no churches to support him; and be is willing to go anywhere he can make a living for himself and wife. I know of many churches in Tennessee and Kentucky who would do well to get him. V. M. Metcalfe.[165]

The report reveals the determination of the small band of Christians at that place. They had purchased a lot and intended to build a house of worship. With Rorex's energy and desire for the work to succeed and Breaker's periodical return trips the work had to be founded upon a solid foundation. The church was established, however so small, and it would succeed.

They were so desirous of preaching that they were taken by a man claiming to be a preacher, but his actions said otherwise. The following report was addressed to "whom it may concern" and tells the sad story:

This is to certify that one S. J Gahagan, who has a letter from the church of Christ at Chattanooga, Tennessee, on or about October 10th, 1883, got drunk at Scottsboro, Ala., and skipped his board and other bills, and has not made any arrangements, as we know of yet, to pay them. We therefore warn the brethren at large to look out for him. November 20, 1883, W. J. Rorex, D. D. S. John B. Harris.[166]

We noticed that another male, John B. Harris, signed his name to the alert. Had he moved to Scottsboro from somewhere else or was he converted recently? We do not know what became of S. J. Gahagan. Nothing else about him was ever printed in the pages of the *Gospel Advocate*. The name Gahagan was found among preachers of Alabama written by J. M. Barnes, but no given name was in the report.[167]

By January 1891 James A. Harding was conducting a gospel meeting in Scottsboro. He planned on staying there for several days since he had his address changed to Scottsboro, Alabama, and published in the January 30 *Gospel Advocate*.[168]

James A. Harding held a meeting in Scottsboro shortly after the Gahagan incident. The *Gospel Advocate* reported the meeting as follows:

> Bro. J. A. Harding says, "We had a fine meeting at Scottsboro. Had eleven additions and started on foot the building of a house." Bro. Harding can be addressed at Winchester, Ky., until further notice.
>
> Bro. J. A. Harding is at Scottsboro, Alabama, where he may be addressed until further notice.[169]

He intended on staying in North Alabama throughout the winter. He desired to preach in places where there were no churches. He had a brother Daugherty leading singing in all of his meetings.[170]

Harding's meeting opened the door for more people in Scottsboro to understand the difference between immersion and sprinkling in the New Testament. He issues a challenge to L. F. Whitten, who waited for Harding to leave town before he challenged Harding's lessons. So, Harding issued a challenge to Whitten for a public debate. His challenge was never answered.

He created quite an uproar among the Methodists and Presbyterians over immersion as opposed to sprinkling or pouring. Harding's report below shows their reactions:

Our teaching at Scottsboro, Ala. stirred up the Paedo-baptist ministers of the place wonderfully. Especially were they annoyed when the people began to understand that sprinkling is not baptism. When they became excited and began to talk about my teaching, I heartily invited them to meet me before the public and discuss the points of difference; or to bring some champion of their cause to the town, who would be willing to undertake their defence. But with great dignity they declined to do any such thing. Since I left, however, I understand that Bro. L. F. Whitten, of the Methodist church has been endeavoring to make the impression that some statement, or statements of mine are false. I stated that Prof. Milton W. Humphreys, professor of Greek in Vanderbilt, says that no standard Greek English lexicon gives sprinkle or pour as a meaning of baptizo. Of this statement I understand Bro. Whitten has endeavored to make some capital. Well; I have in my possession Prof. Humphreys' letter to Bro. L. N. Johnson, in which he makes the statement. He claims that some lexicons give the definition, but no standard Greek-English lexicon does. I say that no respectable lexicographer gives or ever has given "sprinkle" as a definition of baptizo.

If Bro. Whitten wants to expose my teaching to the people of Scottsboro, let him find a man to represent his cause, and I will gladly meet him before the community. I think it appears a little cowardly for him to make such violent attacks after I have left the town. [James A. Harding][171]

In July, a word of encouragement came to some North Alabama congregations, including Scottsboro, who were still struggling to build a house of worship. The message came from the most unlikely place—Meaford, Canada. It read as follows:

The church at Meaford, Canada., where I am now engaged in a meeting, met to break bread for the first time about thirty years ago. There were six members in all at that time. It was about ten years before they had a meeting house; yet in all these years they have not failed to meet, except perhaps on one or two occasions. The church has not employed a pastor to take charge of it in all these years; but for a year or two they sustained Bro. H. B. Sherman as evangelist. The little congregations that are struggling without meetinghouses at Huntsville, Scottsboro and Gadsden, Ala., and at Savannah, Ga. should take courage from this example.[172]

J. W. Shepherd came to Scottsboro and held a meeting that began on September 21, 1884. We do not know the duration of the meeting. We do know that it ended before October 15, 1884. Shepherd had told the *Gospel Advocate* that the meeting would "continue for some time." W. J. Rorex gave a detailed report on the meeting:

Dear Bro. Harding: Bro. J. W. Shepherd began a meeting at the Baptist church here, on September 21, which closed last night. Twenty were added to the Lord – seventeen by baptism, and three reclaimed. Sectarian opposition ran high. Having heard of our intention to begin a meeting, they began a union meeting at the Presbyterian church, on Tuesday night before, after having just closed a meeting of six weeks, resulting in one profession; and as soon as they saw we were having a good hearing from the country some two or three miles away, they sent one of their preachers out to a schoolhouse in order to begin a meeting, and, if possible, checkmate us in that quarter, while the other continued the meeting in town. Also, I understand that they tried to get their Baptist friends to turn us out of their house.

I know you will be glad to hear of the above results, I mean the results of our meeting,) and that we are continuing our Lord's day meeting. We meet each Lord's day to break bread, and to address the things spoken of Paul.

Now, as you come south, can't you call and see us? You can do great good here now. Almost everyone I meet asks me when Bro. Harding is coming back. Bro. Shepherd, however, had all the time a large and attentive audience. He is a man who is able to present and defend the truth, and to expose error. Hoping to hear from you soon, I am, dear sir, yours in the one hope, Scottsboro, Alabama. W. J. Rorex.[173]

This report gave a very good insight into the religious opposition the church at Scottsboro would face. The Presbyterians and Methodists (Paedo-baptist) opposed Shepherd's meeting strongly. The Baptists were gracious toward our brethren, at least for then. Despite the opposition from the Paedo-baptist, Shepherd helped the congregation grow in number with God's help and his clear practical preached sermons. From Rorex's comments, it was apparent that Harding had made an impression on the people in Scottsboro. Rorex had said that—"Almost everyone I meet asks me when Bro. Harding is coming back." This suggested that Harding was well-liked by many in Scottsboro.[174]

By July 1885, the brethren were trying to raise funds to build their house of worship. Sister E. L. Rorex wrote of having received five dollars from a brother in Texas "to help us build our house at Scottsboro, Ala."[175]

In 1890 the congregation was looking forward to having T. W. Brents come and hold a meeting for them. Sister S. D. Gregory sent a very short report to the *Gospel Advocate* that read:

> Our congregation is still small, but we have Lord's day meeting if there are only five. We are expecting Dr. Brents to hold a meeting for us soon. Scottsboro, Oct. 16, '90. Mrs. S. D. Gregory.[176]

Later a report on Brent's meeting was given by B. S. Gowen. It was a thorough picture of Brent's meeting and the Scottsboro work. We give the full article:

> Dr. Brents has just closed a meeting here. For eight days he did some of the strongest preaching of his life. The people here, as a rule, are not bitterly prejudiced, but are certainly ignorant as to

our teaching; they hold some very incorrect views. Our trouble was in getting them out to hear Dr. Brents. When a man came once, he usually came again Some members of other churches never missed a sermon, and some outsiders who do not usually attend church, were present every time. Everything seemed against us. Two concerts and a democratic rally occurred the week of our meeting. Under these circumstances, it was a week before the town realized what a strong man was preaching. The audiences, though small at first, were appreciative. They continued to increase till the night of the close when a large crowd was present. That time had been set for closing, or we would have gone on. We think now it was a mistake but will try to make amends by having another meeting before a great while. Some of the leading members of the sects were actually surprised to know that we insist on faith and repentance, or anything, in fact, except baptism. It was said by one, that if all our preachers preached like Dr. Brents, in less than twenty years, the whole church would go over to the Baptists. But they claim he is the only one that preaches that way. Verily they see we are not the heretics they thought us. We hope that soon, they may be taught the way of the Lord more perfectly B. S. Gowen. Scottsboro, Nov. 15, '90.[177]

The next communication comes through the pages of the *Gospel Advocate* in December 1891. That report stated that the church had sold their building and it had been turned into a town hall and theater. The news was included in a question to David Lipscomb. Lipscomb responds to the question:

We have sold our church building to a company which has made a town hall of it and use it as a theater. In the meantime, the church holds its Lord's day meetings in it until a new house can be built. Some of the members, (and good ones, too,) will not meet with us because the house is used as a theater. Are we doing wrong to meet in it?

This is not intended for publication but would like to have it answered through the Advocate.

I heard a brother remark the other day that the Advocate is the best paper published anywhere. May success and good attend it, is the wish of Nov. 2nd, 1891. Mrs. J. H. Gregory. Scottsboro, Ala.

... The trouble with these good brethren is they are more anxious to follow their prejudices than to obey God. They are willing to set at naught a command of God, and forsake the assembling together, neglect the holding in memory the blood and body of the son of God, which are plainly commanded, to gratify a whim and prejudice for which they can find no Bible authority. It is a clear case of making of none effect the commandments of God, by their traditions or prejudices. We are nowhere in the Bible told we shall not meet where theaters are held nor that we are to meet in houses held sacred. We have the example that they met in private houses and public halls ... D. L. [178]

Had the church outgrown their first building, or had they been offered a better deal and hopefully improve their meeting-house situation? We can only wonder. A new building would be built eventually. Preachers kept coming by and preaching a few sermons, and about twice a year they would have a gospel meeting.

One of the preachers who preached often was Scottsboro's own. Lipscomb was rather proud of him. He had attended the Nashville Bible School. The young man was J. D. Gunn who grew to manhood in Scottsboro. Lipscomb said of him: "He is preaching with good hearing in that section." D. Lipscomb. [179]

In August W. H. Sheffer of Bell Buckle, Tennessee wrote that he intended to come to Scottsboro and hold a meeting. Nothing else was ever said about the meeting—not even the tiniest report. We do not know if Sheffer came or if the meeting was canceled. We know nothing about it. [180]

The church at Scottsboro was generous to other causes. They were contributing to R. W. Officer's work among the Indians of Texas and Oklahoma. They had contributed to other congregations trying to build a house of worship. An example of their generosity toward Officer is below:

> Enclosed you will find $5 for Brother Officer's mission. We have only about a dozen men, women, and children who attend the Lord's-day school, and this is their offering. Hope we will do better in the future. Praying for the success of the ADVOCATE and its editors — Mrs. J. H. Gregory, Scottsboro, Ala., Feb. 20.
> [181]

It must be remembered that in 1894 five dollars could have bought an acre of land in some states. Their donation was generous at that point in history.

Not much occurred during the period from 1894 and 1897. We find only short report relating to the work at Scottsboro and that was concerning a meeting held by J. W. Shepherd. The report simply stated that "Brother J. W. Shepherd recently held a meeting of eight days at Scottsboro, Ala., with one baptism."[182] That was the sum of reporting done between 1894 and 1897.

In March 1897, an alarm was sounded from Scottsboro through the pages of the *Gospel Advocate*. A man claiming the name Link came to Scottsboro and ran a swindle on the church in that place. The details are as follows:

> We have heard of a man by the name of Link claiming to be an agent for the Gospel Advocate. He has collected money from brethren at Scottsboro, Ala., and perhaps at other places. He has never reported the collections to us. He has no authority to act as agent. Brethren should not pay their dues to such men. Link wrote us for an agency. We wrote him at Mooresville, Ala., declining to give him one. He did not receive the letter, as it was returned to us.

Brethren beware of parties claiming to be agents. We mention our regular traveling agents frequently in the columns of the Advocate, besides giving each a letter of recommendation. This does not apply to local agents who are well known where they work.[183]

It appears Scottsboro attracted a drunken preacher who did not pay his bills and a fraud artist who claimed to be something he was not. Scottsboro was growing to maturity as a strong congregation. Its spiritual condition was very good, and the members were striving to grow into the way the Lord desires a congregation to be. This is demonstrated in the next communication. J. H. Gregory sent an inquiry to Lipscomb about Christians holding public office. It reads:

> Brother Lipscomb: The devil tempted our Savior by offering him the kingdoms of this world, which he refused to accept, and as we have no account of Satan giving them to anyone else, it is fair to presume that he still owns them. Now, can a man be a loyal citizen of the kingdom of Christ and at the same time hold an office under one of these kingdoms? I am holding an office by appointment of the Governor of my State, and am desirous of retaining it, if I can do so and still be loyal to the kingdom of Christ. Can any brother help me along this line? Scottsboro, Ala. J. H. Gregory.[184]

Gregory seemed to really struggling with this; but he also seemed to indicate that if he were in the wrong, he would correct the situation. That is Christian maturity!

A few weeks after Gregory's communication brothers R. H. Boll and E. E. Sewell came to North Alabama and preached during the summer. Boll had preached at various locations all summer and Sewell preached for three weeks. They ended their summer meetings with one at Scottsboro. They described Scottsboro as:

A destitute field, in which the gospel has been little preached, and these brethren are to be commended for their efforts to plant the truth in this section.[185]

Boll was a staff member at the *Gospel Advocate* at the time he came to Scottsboro, but later he would be dismissed from the *Gospel Advocate*. He began to hold premillennial views and teach them. At the time he was in Scottsboro, he did not teach this doctrine. He later moved to Louisville, Kentucky where he caused quite a stir.

T. A. Smith came in October and preached twelve sermons at Scottsboro, and one of them was on the fifth Sunday of October. Smith gave a report concerning the meeting and revealed some things about the church at Scottsboro:

... Six persons confessed their faith in Christ; five were baptized, and one was to be baptized by Brother Kirk in a day or two. Scottsboro is a nice town, of about twelve hundred inhabitants. They have a fine normal college, and the outlook is good for a fine school. The church is true to the old gospel, having a number of faithful, intelligent brethren and sisters. With more zeal there is a bright future before them. Brother Kirk lives nearby. He was with me in almost every service, assisting in prayers and worship. He is a faithful preacher, doing much good, and is held in high esteem in the regions around, as well as at home, so I learned ... T. A. Smith.[186]

This gave another boost of spiritual energy. Brother J. H. Gregory did his part in a two-fold effort to help both the church and the town get more Christians. His effort is demonstrated in the following report. He wrote:

A saddler and harness maker, who is a member of the church of God, is wanted to locate at Scottsboro, Ala. There is a fine open-

ing, and no opposition. Address J. H. Gregory, Scottsboro, Ala.
[187]

Gregory had become one of the leaders in the church at Scottsboro. Brother W. J. Rorex, who had been a leader in the founding days had relocated to Stevenson by 1900 and was a leading figure there. So, now Gregory was in a leadership role. His love for the church and Christ cannot be mistaken. If all the members in Scottsboro had the energy Gregory had the church would have grown rapidly. He would continue trying to persuade Christians to move to Scottsboro, especially those with a set of trade skills. In that way, the church would grow, and the town would benefit by gaining a new trade for the town.

The brethren had become protective of David Lipscomb in some ways. Even with Lipscomb's curt answers the people still valued his wisdom in church affairs. A brother R. S. Crews demonstrated this in a short message to Lipscomb:

> Brother Lipscomb: There is a Methodist preacher stationed at Scottsboro, Ala., who made the assertion this week that Dave Lipscomb and the whole Gospel Advocate force denounced the Old Testament as a back number and would not take n text and discuss a subject from it. For the benefit of some weak brethren at. Scottsboro. please write a short article in the Advocate on. what you believe concerning the Old Testament. R. S. Crews.[188]

Lipscomb was the main reason the *Gospel Advocate* was so trusted. Lipscomb, like Alexander Campbell, would ignore many of the slanderous remarks made about him.

In October 1902 E. A. Elam began a meeting at Scottsboro on the fourth Sunday of October.[189] No report of this meeting could be found in the *Gospel Advocate*.

In November J. H. Gregory made another one of his "church and town" improvement appeals in the *Gospel Advocate*. He was trying to persuade a Christian who had skills in woodworking on wagons and buggies, to relocate to Scottsboro.[190]

News from Scottsboro was scant during the first decade of the 1900s. Messages came from Scottsboro, but they were appeals or questions to the *Gospel Advocate*. Not much real information about the church. Another appeal came from Gregory, but this one was a little different from the other appeals. This one was not asking for someone to relocate to Scottsboro, but rather requesting that E. A. Elam produce a tract on the subject of the "Digressive Movement." The *Gospel Advocate* agreed that Elam was the right man to write a tract on that subject.[191]

In keeping with the scanty news from Scottsboro during the first decade of the twentieth century, it was three more years before another bit of information came. This message reveals another characteristic about Gregory and the church. He expressed his gratitude to the *Gospel Advocate* for its content and asked them to send the paper to some deserving widow. He had enclosed a dollar and a half to cover the subscription. Gregory really manifested the Christian spirit.[192]

Late in of 1906 A. B. Blazer came and preached on the last Sunday of April at Scottsboro.[193] Blazer was a native of Jackson County. He grew to manhood in the Rocky Springs area. He would come back and preach many times during his lifetime.

In November of that year, J. H. Gregory made another appeal for a Christian dentist to move to Scottsboro and set up a practice. He said in his request: "No doubt this is a good opening for the right man."[194] Brother Gregory was always looking for the right man to relocate to Scottsboro and work. If all of his appeals were answered Scottsboro would have a heavy population of Christian businessmen.

On January 13, 1907, A. B. Blazer came on another visit to Scottsboro and preached.[195] He reported that he preached in Scottsboro again on March 3rd.[196] He also stated that J. A. Harding was returning to Scottsboro for a gospel meeting. Blazer's reports of his preaching at Scottsboro indicate that he had a circuit of churches for which he preached on a regular basis. He never was one for sending many reports on his work. He just did the work. His son Howard Blazer, Sr., who would be born about two years later, followed in his father's footsteps. This writer personally knew brother Howard Blazer.

That old problem appeared again in Scottsboro. Another swindle artist shows up in town and of course, came to some of the members of the church who became his victims. J. H. Gregory sounded the alarm:

> Brother J. H. Gregory, of Scottsboro, Ala., writes under date of May 27: "One John J. Mastin, a man with a wooden leg, has been here. claiming to be a gospel preacher and a lecturer on the Holy Land. He preached at Carthage and Harriman. Tenn., as a Baptist preacher. He obtained money from me on a worthless draft." We have been informed that this same John J. Mastin has been preaching at Tracy City, Tenn.[197]

The brethren at Scottsboro were so anxious to do good deeds that sometimes scammers took advantage of their good nature. That is what happened with the peg-legged man. Even brother Rorex, a good businessman lets himself be defrauded. The brethren of Scottsboro knew that God would take care of them as long as they did was with the best of intentions, when it came to trying to do the right thing toward others.

Nearly two years went by without a communication from Scottsboro. Sometime in April 1909 Brother L. B. Lucas, of Bridgeport, Ala., came and preached. He baptized four persons. [198]

On the second week of May 1909 W. T. Boaz of Columbia, Tennessee held a meeting for the brethren at Scottsboro. The same old story repeated—no final report on the meeting. It is possible that Lucas, having baptized four souls just two weeks prior to Boaz's meeting, had baptized, at that time, all who were at that high point, spiritually, in their lives. That would have made

Boaz's job more difficult in converting a lost soul. Whatever the situation—Boaz never reported on the meeting. In fairness to Boaz, he was a very good preacher and highly desired as a meeting preacher.

In the middle of the year 1910, an invitation was sent to Brother J. M. McCaleb, a missionary to Japan, to come to Scottsboro and preach. This is his report:

> Sister Gregory last January wrote me, asking if I could come to Scottsboro, Ala. I found I could run down there from Stevenson, a distance of eighteen miles. We had two interesting meetings on June 8 and 9. While here I was the guest of Brother and Sister Gregory, and everything possible was done to make my stay pleasant and comfortable. J. M. McCaleb.[199]

This report reflected some of that "Good Ole Southern Hospitality." The Gregory home was always open to Christians who passed through their town.

About a week after McCaleb's visit, F. W. Smith came and conducted a gospel meeting. The *Gospel Advocate* reported the following:

> Brother F. W. Smith's meeting at Scottsboro, Ala., closed with nine additions-five baptized, one restored, one from the Baptists. and two "by membership." The attendance throughout the meeting was the best for many years.[200]

This meeting gave another incentive to continue working hard for the cause of Christ in their town. Brother Gregory, in his energetic way, once more makes another appeal for Christians who are looking for work to come to Scottsboro. The following appeared in the October 13 edition of the *Gospel Advocate*:

> The brethren at Scottsboro, Ala., are very anxious to get brethren and sisters who desire to change their location to locate

there. In order to get In communication with those who contemplate a change, Brother J. H. Gregory, of that place, requests us to publish the following: "Scottsboro, county seat or Jackson County, Ala., is a town of about twelve hundred inhabitants—an educated and refined people. It has five splendid pikes running into it; a State high school and city school, tuition free, the buildings for which cost twenty-five thousand dollars. Lands are the same quality as in Middle Tennessee at less than half the price here. It has a faithful congregation of disciples. Any brother desiring to make a change in location, should address me."[201]

By the middle of 1911 a young preacher, who had studied at the Nashville Bible School, moved to Scottsboro, maybe an answer to Gregory's appeal? The young man was J. M. Gainer. The *Gospel Advocate* said of him:

J. M. Gainer is doing some fine work at Scottsboro, Ala. He is one of our most promising young preachers, and we shall expect nothing but good reports from him. He says he talks for the school at every opportunity.[202]

It seemed that Scottsboro had its first located preacher. Gainer, however, would do preaching in the surrounding areas. He would be able to help strengthen some of the smaller congregations within the Scottsboro region of Jackson County.

In October W. T. Boaz returned and conducted another meeting. This time he baptized one person. It was proclaimed a "good meeting."[203] It would be more than a year before any more information would come forth from Scottsboro.

That information would come in another appeal from Brother J. H. Gregory. He appeals to a potential bricklayer to move to Scottsboro. The following shows how Gregory describes things:

Wanted—A brick mason who is a disciple to locate in the county seat of a rich county in the Tennessee River Valley. High schools and city schools with free tuition. Address J. H. Gregory, Scottsboro, Ala.[204]

With a growing town, there was always a need for tradesmen to locate there. Gregory just hopefully wished that they were always Christian tradesmen.

R. W. Jernigan who lived in Bridgeport was going to work under the oversight of the congregation at Bridgeport and the congregation at Scottsboro for 1914. Charles Holder of Bridgeport described as follows:

> The churches at Bridgeport and Scottsboro, Ala., are to use Brother R. W. Jernigan in evangelizing Jackson County, Ala., next year. Brother Jernigan recently gave up school-teaching and located at Bridgeport to do the work of an evangelist. He is a good Another man, a loyal preacher and is doing good. May the Lord bless his work. More and better work for the Lord should be the desire and determination of all. Charles Holder.[205]

Brother J. M. Gainer moved from Scottsboro. Alabama, to Dallas, Texas in 1913.[206] This was possibly the reason Jernigan was hired to work for the Scottsboro and Bridgeport churches in evangelizing the area. Jernigan's labors were not reported in the *Gospel Advocate* for 1913. We have no clue as to how successful his labors were.

In December 1913, another appeal was published by the *Gospel Advocate* on behalf of J. H. Gregory. He was trying to entice a Christian who was a butcher to come to Scottsboro. Except for the report of Gainer's removable to Texas, which would be the only communication from Scottsboro for the year. [207]

In 1914 William Klingman and R. W Jernigan began a meeting a meeting in Scottsboro, Ala., on June 7. Klingman conducted the singing and Jernigan did the preaching. It was reported that good crowds attended both day and evening services. Three were baptized. Jernigan said:

> The church is waking up to a greater field of usefulness. They have lately installed four hundred and fifty dollars' worth of new seats and will soon repair their house. Scottsboro and our home congregation will keep us in the field all the summer and fall. My wife was with us in this meeting and will always remember the kindness shown her. We are now at home with a sick child. Pray for us. R. W. Jernigan.[208]

That was the last communication relating to the work in Scottsboro within our parameters of time (1914). This closes our study on the church in Scottsboro. It would survive and become the leading congregation in Jackson County. Many great works would emanate from there and many young men would grow up under the influence of the congregation and become good gospel preachers.

Along with our study of the Scottsboro work ending, this also ends our study of the Jackson County movement. Our parameter of time was 1811 to 1914. That would be the actual date from the establishment of the Rocky Springs congregation until the beginning of World War I. Jackson County has a very colorful Restoration Movement history—one that impacted not only North Alabama; but also, other states as well.

ENDNOTES

[1] Ernest A. Clevenger, Jr. @ *Any Age: An Autobiographical Memoir With Genealogical and Historical Records*, (s.l.: Clevenger, 2011).

[2] Wendell Anderson Jacobs, editor and compiler, *Church of Christ History: Area Chattanooga, TN* ([Trenton, Georgia?] : [Wendell A. Jacobs, 1978), 10.

[3] Hall, *Autobiography*, 59–60.

[4] Hall, *Autobiography*, 57–58.

[5] A photocopy of the original Ordination Certificate, February 12, 1827.

[6] *Christian Messenger* (October 25, 1827), 276–277.

[7] A photocopy of the original Ordination Certificate, February 4, 1828.

[8] *Marriage Book–1829*, Limestone County, Alabama. Note: This is the certificate issued on Feb. 4, 1828.

[9] *Gospel Advocate* (June 26, 1902), 408.

[10] *Christian Messenger* (March 1832), 94.

[11] *Christian Messenger* (September 1833), 287.

[12] *Gospel Advocate* (May 9, 1867), 365.

[13] *Gospel Advocate* (August 8, 1867), 638.

[14] *Gospel Advocate* (August 29, 1867), 700.

[15] *Gospel Advocate* (February 6, 1868), 134.

[16] *Gospel Advocate* (July 13, 1868), 765–766.

[17] *Gospel Advocate* (December 9, 1869), 1120–1121.

[18] *Gospel Advocate* (August 12, 1885), 504.

[19] *Gospel Advocate* (May 5, 1885), 275.

[20] *Gospel Advocate* (February 5, 1890), 83.

[21] *Gospel Advocate* (September 22, 1892), 601.

[22] *Gospel Advocate* (December 14, 1893), 789.

[23] *Gospel Advocate* (March 14, 1895), 176.

[24] *Gospel Advocate* (September 24, 1896), 620.

[25] *Gospel Advocate* (September 3, 1896), 572.

[26] *Gospel Advocate* (September 3, 1896), 572.

[27] *Gospel Advocate* (December 24, 1896), 829.

[28] *Gospel Advocate* (December 24, 1896), 829.

[29] *Gospel Advocate* (November 4, 1897), 696.

[30] The 1826 date is confirmed by the first given by Rocky Springs on February 12, 1827. Anderson was baptized six months before this certificate was issued.

[31] *Gospel Advocate* (June 26, 1902), 408.

[32] *Gospel Advocate* (June 26, 1902), 408.

[33] *Gospel Advocate* (November 2, 1916), 1097.

[34] *Gospel Advocate* (October 1, 1908), 629.

[35] *Gospel Advocate* (August 6, 1909), 980.

[36] *Gospel Advocate* (November 11, 1909), 1436.

[37] *Gospel Advocate* (January 18, 1912), 87.

[38] *Gospel Advocate* (July 2, 1914), 734.

[39] *Gospel Advocate* (December 30, 1915), 1324.

[40] Hall, *Autobiography*, 55–57.

[41] *Gospel Advocate* (May 8, 1889), 296.

[42] *Gospel Advocate* (March 14, 1895), 176.

[43] *Gospel Advocate* (September 24, 1896), 620.

[44] *Gospel Advocate* (August 29, 1867), 700.

[45] *Gospel Advocate* (December 9, 1869), 1120–21.

[46] *Gospel Advocate* (December 17, 1874), 1187.

[47] *Gospel Advocate* (January 11, 1883), 21.

[48] *Gospel Advocate* (September 7, 1882), 571.

[49] *Gospel Advocate* (October 19, 1882), 660.

[50] *Gospel Advocate* (June 24, 1885), 386.

[51] *Gospel Advocate* (June 24, 1885), 386.

[52] *Gospel Advocate* (December 18, 1873), 1207.

[53] *Gospel Advocate* (October 14, 1875), 983.

[54] *Gospel Advocate* (May 31, 1923), 540–1.

[55] *Gospel Advocate* (December 17, 1874), 1187.

[56] *Gospel Advocate* (September 9, 1875), 863.

[57] *Gospel Advocate* (October 14, 1875), 934.

[58] *Gospel Advocate* (June 17, 1876), 599.

[59] *Gospel Advocate* (October 19, 1876), 1019.

[60] *Gospel Advocate* (September 19, 1912), 1056.

[61] *Gospel Advocate* (November 31, 1883), 743.

[62] *Gospel Advocate* (February 27, 1884), 132.

[63] *Gospel Advocate* (April 29, 1885), 263.

[64] *Gospel Advocate* (May 5, 1885), 275.

[65] *Gospel Advocate* (June 2, 1886), 347.

[66] *Gospel Advocate* (September 22, 1886), 603.

[67] *Gospel Advocate* (September 22, 1886), 603.

[68] *Gospel Advocate* (September 22, 1886), 603.

[69] *Gospel Advocate* (November 10, 1886), 710.

[70] *Gospel Advocate* (November 10, 1886), 710.

[71] *Gospel Advocate* (June 9, 1886), 354.

[72] *Gospel Advocate* (July 21, 1886), 456.

[73] *Gospel Advocate* (July 21, 1886), 456.

[74] *Gospel Advocate* (March 16, 1944), 194.

[75] *Gospel Advocate* (July 1992), 34.

[76] *Gospel Advocate* (September 2004), 41.

[77] *Gospel Advocate* (November 10, 1886), 710.

[78] *A Short History of the Bridgeport Church of Christ*, 1.

[79] *Gospel Advocate* (Sept. 3, 1896), 572.

[80] *Gospel Advocate* (September 24, 1896), 620.

[81] Flossie Carmichael and Ronald Lee, *In And Around Bridgeport*, Collegedale, TN: College Press, n.d.), 78.

[82] *Gospel Advocate* (November 11, 1909), 1436.

[83] *Gospel Advocate* (November 27, 1913), 1161.

[84] *Gospel Advocate* (June 4, 1914), 616.

[85] *Gospel Advocate* (September 13), 1894, 582.

[86] *Gospel Advocate* (September 5, 1895), 572.

[87] *Gospel Advocate* (August 13, 1896), 525.

[88] *Gospel Advocate* (Sept. 3, 1896), 572.

[89] *Gospel Advocate* (October 19, 1899), 671.

[90] *Gospel Advocate* (August 24, 1905), 540.

[91] *Gospel Advocate* (August 5, 1909), 980.

[92] *Gospel Advocate* (November 11, 1909), 1436.

[93] *Gospel Advocate* (September 1, 1919).

[94] *Gospel Advocate* (September 5, 1901), 572.

[95] *Gospel Advocate* (October 2, 1902), 629.

[96] *Gospel Advocate* (October 30, 1902), 693.

[97] *Gospel Advocate* (November 6, 1902), .703.

[98] *Gospel Advocate* (October 6, 1905), 636.

[99] *Gospel Advocate* (September 5, 1910), 1024.

[100] *Gospel Advocate* (March 23, 1911), 358.

[101] *Gospel Advocate* (October 12, 1911,) 636.

[102] *Gospel Advocate* (August 29, 1912), 981.

[103] *Gospel Advocate* (April 24, 1913), 396.

[104] *Gospel Advocate* (September 11, 1913), 879.

[105] *Gospel Advocate* (March 29, 1917), 322.

[106] *Gospel Advocate* (August 6, 1925), 756.

[107] *Gospel Advocate* (October 21, 1885), 667.

[108] *Gospel Advocate* (August 7, 1889), 499.

[109] *Gospel Advocate* (November 7, 1912), 1221.

[110] *Gospel Advocate* (October 17, 1912), 1148.

[111] *Gospel Advocate* (September 11, 1913), 879.

[112] *Gospel Advocate* (April 2, 1914), 373.

[113] *Gospel Advocate* (June 11, 1914), 647.

[114] *Gospel Advocate* (July 16, 1914), 776.

[115] *Gospel Advocate* (July 23, 1914), 805.

[116] *Gospel Advocate* (November 4, 1897), 695.

[117] *Gospel Advocate* (October 1, 1896), 636.

[118] *Gospel Advocate* (October 15, 1896), 668.

[119] *Gospel Advocate* (August 12, 1897), 508.

[120] *Gospel Advocate* (November 4, 1897), 695.

[121] *Gospel Advocate* (November 25, 1897), 749.

[122] (*Gospel Advocate* (December 26, 1897), 797.

[123] *Gospel Advocate* (September 21, 1899), 605.

[124] *Deed Book, Lincoln County, Tennessee, 1900,* 284.

[125] *Gospel Advocate* (May 31, 1906), 341.

[126] *Gospel Advocate* (May 24, 1906), 336.

[127] *Gospel Advocate* (September 20, 1900), 604.

[128] *Gospel Advocate* (September 27, 1900), 620.

[129] *Gospel Advocate* (September 5, 1901), 572.

[130] *Gospel Advocate* (September 1, 1910), 996.

[131] *Gospel Advocate* (July 18, 1907), 453.

[132] *Gospel Advocate* (September 1, 1910), 996.

[133] *Gospel Advocate* (October 10, 1912), 1124.

[134] *Gospel Advocate* (September 11, 1913), 879.

[135] *Gospel Advocate* (July 20, 1893), 457.

[136] *Gospel Advocate* (August 24, 1893), 533.

[137] *Gospel Advocate* (August 19, 1897), 518.

[138] *Gospel Advocate* (August 19, 1897), 518.

[139] *Gospel Advocate* (July 26, 1900), 469.

[140] *Gospel Advocate* (April 12, 1906), 229.

[141] *Gospel Advocate* (September 26, 1901), 619.

[142] *Gospel Advocate* (July 31, 1902), 492.

[143] *Gospel Advocate* (July 26, 1900), 469; *Gospel Advocate* (July 31, 1902), 492.

[144] *Gospel Advocate* (July 7, 1904), 431.

[145] *Gospel Advocate* (July 7, 1904), 431.

[146] *Gospel Advocate* (April 12, 1906), 229.

[147] *Gospel Advocate* (September 20, 1906), 597.

[148] *Gospel Advocate* (February 7, 1907), 88.

[149] *Gospel Advocate* (April 18, 1907), 254.

[150] *Gospel Advocate* (March 4, 1909), 283.

[151] *Gospel Advocate* (March 4, 1909), 283.

[152] *Gospel Advocate* (May 6, 1909), 561.

[153] *Gospel Advocate* (May 6, 1909), 575.

[154] *Gospel Advocate* (January 6, 1910), 20.

[155] *Gospel Advocate* (March 31, 1910), 389.

[156] *Gospel Advocate* (March 31, 1910), 389.

[157] *Gospel Advocate* (July 14, 1910), 819.

[158] *Gospel Advocate* (July 17, 1913), 685.

[159] *Gospel Advocate* (December 11, 1913), 1215.

[160] *Gospel Advocate* (July 2, 1914), 729.

[161] *Gospel Advocate* (October 22, 1914), 1108.

[162] *Gospel Advocate* (November 9, 1882), 715.

[163] *Gospel Advocate* (December 7, 1882), 775.

[164] *Gospel Advocate* (December 7, 1882), 774–5.

[165] *Gospel Advocate* (January 18, 1883), 41.

[166] *Gospel Advocate* (December 19, 1883), 802.

[167] *Gospel Advocate* (January 9, 1884), 23.

[168] *Gospel Advocate* (January 30, 1884), 75.

[169] *Gospel Advocate* (January 30, 1884), 75.

[170] *Gospel Advocate* (January 30, 1884), 75.

[171] *Gospel Advocate* (April 2, 1884), 218.

[172] *Gospel Advocate* (July 16, 1884), 458.

[173] *Gospel Advocate* (October 15, 1884), 666.

[174] *Gospel Advocate* (October 15, 1884), 666.

[175] *Gospel Advocate* (July 29, 1885), 470.

[176] *Gospel Advocate* (October 29, 1890), 691.

[177] *Gospel Advocate* (November 26, 1890), 755.

[178] *Gospel Advocate* (December 10, 1891), 781.

[179] *Gospel Advocate* (July 21, 1892), 456.

[180] *Gospel Advocate* (September 1, 1892), 556.

[181] *Gospel Advocate* (March 1, 1894), 136.

[182] *Gospel Advocate* (May 9, 1895), 296.

[183] *Gospel Advocate* (March 1, 1897), 152.

[184] *Gospel Advocate* (September 8, 1898), 573.

[185] *Gospel Advocate* (September 29, 1898), 617.

[186] *Gospel Advocate* (December 7, 1899), 781.
[187] *Gospel Advocate* (October 25, 1900), 677.
[188] *Gospel Advocate* (September 12, 1901), 579.
[189] *Gospel Advocate* (October 16, 1902), 661.
[190] *Gospel Advocate* (November 20, 1902), 748.
[191] *Gospel Advocate* (April 16, 1903), 245.
[192] *Gospel Advocate* (January 18, 1906), 37.
[193] *Gospel Advocate* (May 10, 1906), 293.
[194] *Gospel Advocate* (November 22, 1906), 741.
[195] *Gospel Advocate* (January 31, 1907), 69.
[196] *Gospel Advocate* (March 21, 1907), 181.
[197] *Gospel Advocate* (June 6, 1907), 357.
[198] *Gospel Advocate* (May 13, 1909), 592.
[199] *Gospel Advocate* (July 14, 1910), 819.
[200] *Gospel Advocate* (August 11, 1910), 924.
[201] *Gospel Advocate* (October 13, 1910), 1141.
[202] *Gospel Advocate* (July 6, 1911), 741.
[203] *Gospel Advocate* (November 2), 1911, 1264.
[204] *Gospel Advocate* (March 13, 1913), 252.
[205] *Gospel Advocate* (November 27, 1913), 1161.
[206] *Gospel Advocate* (November 27, 1913), 1160.
[207] *Gospel Advocate* (December 18, 1913), 1257.
[208] *Gospel Advocate* (June 25, 1914), 705.

Bibliography

Books

Carmichael, Flossie, and Ronald Lee. *In And Around Bridgeport*. Collegedale, TN: College Press, n.d.

Clevenger, Ernest A., Jr. *@ Any Age: An Autobiographical Memoir With Genealogical and Historical Records*. s.l.: Clevenger, 2011.

Hall, Benjamin Franklin. *Autobiography of Benjamin Franklin Hall*. s.l.: s.n., n.d.

Jacobs, Wendell Anderson, editor and compiler. *Church of Christ History: Area Chattanooga, TN*. [Trenton, Georgia?]:[Wendell A. Jacobs], 1978.

Periodicals

Christian Messenger
Gospel Advocate

Name Index

ALSO BY C. WAYNE KILPATRICK

An Early History of the Mars Hill Church of Christ: With a Collection of Memories by Members of the Congregation (2024)

J. R. Bradley: A Forgotten Larimore Boy (2019)

John Chisholm Church History Series

including

A Little Band of Disciples: The Beginnings of Churches of Christ in Madison County, Alabama

A Faithful Band of Workers: The Beginnings of Churches of Christ in Jackson County, Alabama

A Noble Band of Worshipers: The Beginnings of Churches of Christ Lauderdale County, Alabama

A Small Band of Brethren: The Beginnings of Churches of Christ in Limestone County, Alabama

CYPRESS

To see the full catalog of Heritage Christian University Press and
its imprint, Cypress Publications, visit
www.hcupress.edu

Milton Keynes UK
Ingram Content Group UK Ltd.
UKHW040255291024
450401UK00006B/58